Praise for

Lifelines: Poems for Winslow Homer and Edward Hopper

"As Joseph Stanton well knows and has demonstrated in his various books of ekphrastic poetry, paintings speak. All one has to do is listen. In the poems in this volume, the paintings of Winslow Homer and Edward Hopper speak powerful messages on war, nature, the situations of women, the city, life, love, and death—all to the benefit of the artists and the readers of this impressive book that celebrates both paintings and poetry."

—ROBERT HAMBLIN, author of *Myself and the World: A Biography of William Faulkner*

•

"Joseph Stanton is one of America's most accomplished ekphrastic poets, and in the work of Hopper and Homer he has found subjects that nourish his observant eye and capture his nuanced ear."

—RICHARD WENDORF, Director Emeritus of the Boston Athenaeum, author of *The Elements of Life: Biography and Portrait Painting*

•

"Edward Hopper's paintings have long engaged poets, just as poetry—from Verlaine to Frost—engaged Hopper. Joseph Stanton's poems not only relate to what Hopper painted, but also to the painter's biography. These evocative poems take the reader closer to the essence of Hopper's images and even sometimes to his feisty relationship with his wife, Jo. Hopper himself would not have minded being paired with poems about Winslow Homer, an artist whom he admired."

—GAIL LEVIN, author of *Edward Hopper: An Intimate Biography*

•

"As both an art historian and a poet, Joseph Stanton brings a unique perspective to bear on his thinking about works of art. He has written on a wide range of historic and contemporary art . . . In *Lifelines: Poems for Winslow Homer and Edward Hopper*, Stanton continues to create imaginary exhibitions in literary museums whose contents juxtapose images and provoke ideas. In this installment he focuses on two classic American painters: Winslow Homer and Edward Hopper. Drawing upon his professional experience and aesthetic sense, Stanton gives voice to these silent works of visual art. The poems not only complement each other, but illuminate and deepen our understanding of the paintings. Adding to these reflections on our everyday world are observations regarding the psychology of a simple setting. Whether there are isolated figures sitting in a late-night diner, or a young whippersnapper trailing at the end of a crack-the-whip game, an undeniable tension comes into play. It is this tension, both plastic and poetic, that gives Joseph Stanton's work its unique importance."

—Richard Emery Nickolson, artist and author of the blog *Bridging the Gap: Reflections on the Plastic and Ekphrastic Traditions*

•

"Taking imaginative leaps into the pictures of celebrated American artists Winslow Homer and Edward Hopper, Joseph Stanton pens poems that offer unique revelations about them. Moving through each artist's career one work at a time, roughly in the order they were created, he opens new windows onto their visual imagery with his prescient observations and exquisitely crafted lines. Interpretations of pictorial details lead him to suggest absences and yearnings in their personal lives, which can be intriguing—though tricky—given that both attempted to thwart any invasion of their privacy. Homer's bachelor life, fishing and hunting, between the Civil War and the Spanish American War is differentiated by subtle shifts in vocabulary and poetic style from Hopper's twentieth century primarily urban existence and his complex relationship with his wife, Jo. Stanton's skillful wielding of the ekphrastic stance brings alternative perspectives to the 'so-long-lonely Winslow' and Hopper, 'Puritan by birth, sensualist at heart.' Both seasoned readers of the burgeoning literature on these two revered figures and those just discovering them will be inspired by *Lifelines*."

—KATHERINE MANTHORNE, author of *Film and Modern American Art: The Dialogue Between Cinema and Painting*

•

"*Lifelines: Poems for Winslow Homer and Edward Hopper* develops unexpectedly, like a story, in chronological order, year by year—until the pattern is disrupted. The poems are in the tradition of ekphrasis, with their individual focuses on specific works of art, while taken together they create a kind of art history in/as poetry. The values of the artists' times, not of ours, come to life. Recurring themes of humor, wit, and games are woven throughout the Winslow Homer poems, then echoed in a few of the Edward Hopper poems, including, significantly, the concluding poem, 'Two Comedians, 1965.' This structure, together with Joseph Stanton's, deceptively simple, lucid descriptions throughout, offer a unique vision of how two artists explored life, love, and mortality."

—REVA WOLF, author of *Andy Warhol, Poetry, and Gossip in the 1960s*

•

"Joseph Stanton's *Lifelines: Poems for Winslow Homer and Edward Hopper* trains a keen, informed eye on two iconic American painters, one of them gregarious, bountiful, and engaged, the other enigmatic and distanced. The Winslow Homer poems constitute both a minibiography of the painter and a series of glimpses into American life in the last half of the nineteenth century. With the Hopper poems we enter a changed America, a lapsed world following the Edenic land that Homer registered so vividly. The sparely framed Hopper poems echo the artist's vision of American loneliness, ennui, and unrealized dreams. After reading *Lifelines,* we will forever view these artists through a different lens."

—RICHARD TILLINGHAST, author of
Blue If Only I Could Tell You

•

"A Joseph Stanton collection is always cause for celebration, and this rich poetic examination of two enigmatic American artists is a rich addition to the ekphrastic world. Stanton looks confidently at canvas after canvas, reading scenes and symbols, as well as angles and frames and colors and compositions. Art is a language he speaks fluently as a scholar, and through this poetry he is an artist himself."

—LORETTE LUZAJIC, editor of *The Ekphrastic Review*

•

"These are indeed lifelines—poems covering almost forty years of Homer's paintings and a half-century of Hopper's. Over decades, Joseph Stanton has studied the lives and works of these two artists and written poems about them. What strikes this reader is the shape of the book, both of each half and of the book as a whole. It is uncanny how poems written at different times, but now arranged by the chronology of the paintings, connect each with the next in a kind of natural order. With poet Joseph Stanton as our guide, we can enter into the minds and hearts of these two iconic American artists to see what they see—Homer's natural and human landscapes, Hopper's haunting light and absences—whether or not we have the images in front of us."

—SUE COWING, author of *Call Me Drog*

•

"In his exquisite new collection of poems, Joseph Stanton brings together the worlds of Homer and Hopper, providing every 'stilled moment' with a narrative that springs from a deep understanding of both artists, filling sparse rooms and embattled landscapes with life beyond the canvas. Stanton begins his poem on Homer's *Artists Sketching in the White Mountains* with the line 'Landscape artists must be part of what they see.' The same might be said for ekphrastic poets and, by this measure alone, Stanton never disappoints."

—VALERIE ROBILLARD, author of *The Ekphrastic Moment in the Poetry of William Carlos Williams*

•

"In *Lifelines: Poems for Winslow Homer and Edward Hopper,* Stanton's poems deftly explore visual and thematic clues left by artists Homer and Hopper, and result in fascinating and thought-provoking narratives. His extensive art historical knowledge and creative imagination combined with descriptive language work to immerse the reader in a specific place or moment in time. Stanton is able to access imagined inner thoughts, explore psychological undercurrents, and heighten the expressive mood portrayed in the artworks. This collection of poems makes for an inspiring read that will intrigue both the casual fan and the connoisseur of art history, painting, and poetry."

—KATHERINE LOVE, artist and Assistant Curator of Contemporary Art Honolulu Museum of Art

LIFELINES

LIFELINES

Poems for Winslow Homer and Edward Hopper

Joseph Stanton

Shanti Arts Publishing
Brunswick, Maine

LIFELINES: Poems for Winslow Homer and Edward Hopper

Published by Shanti Arts Publishing

Designed by Shanti Arts Designs

Shanti Arts LLC
193 Hillside Road
Brunswick, Maine 04011
shantiarts.com

Printed in the United States of America

ISBN: 978-1-956056-89-1

Library of Congress Control Number: 2023938873

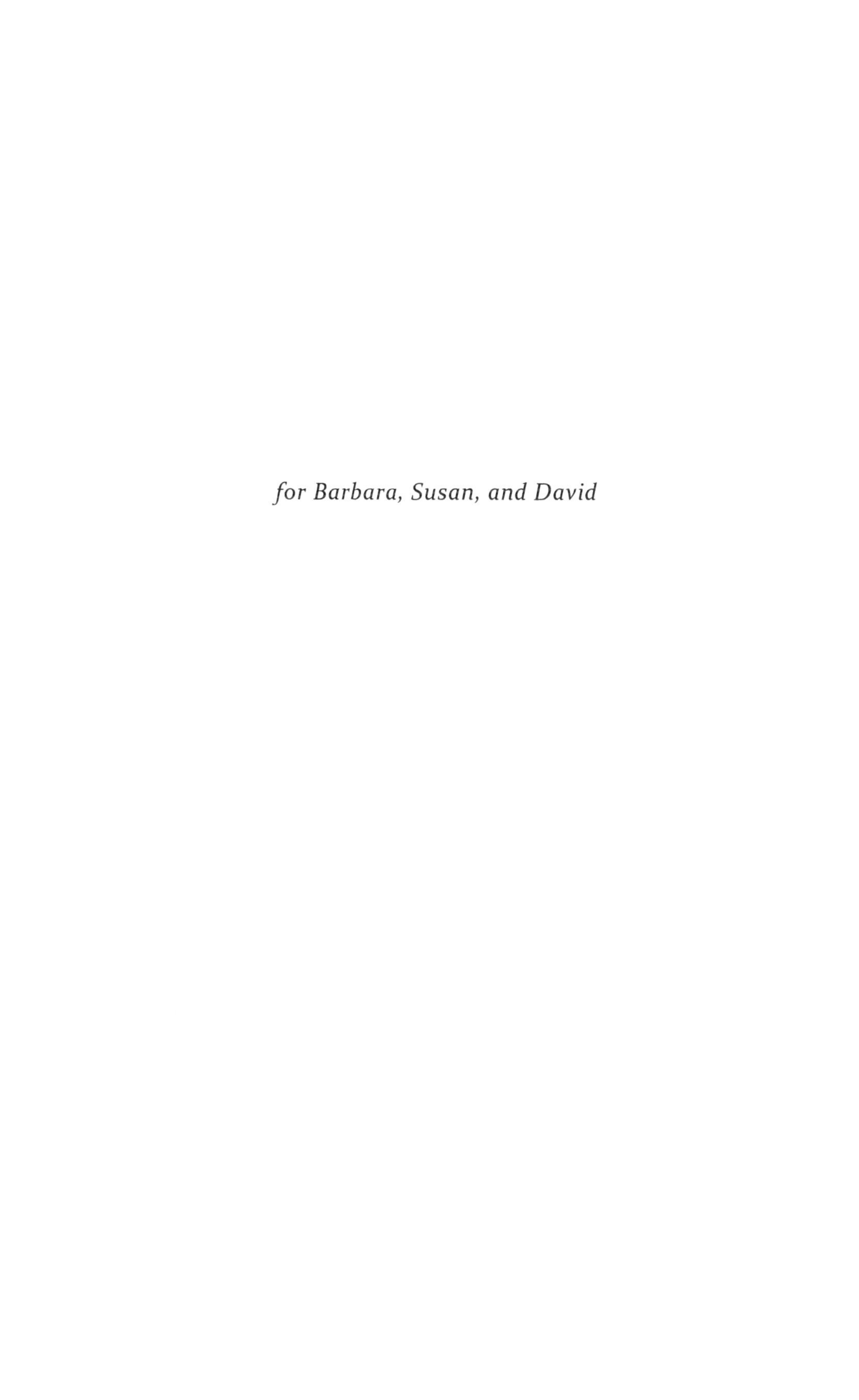

for Barbara, Susan, and David

Contents

EDWARD HOPPER

Information about Artwork Cited

All images that appear in this book are in the public domain.

WINSLOW HOMER

[24, 25] *A Sharpshooter on Picket Duty*, 1862. Wood engraving. Cleveland Museum of Art, Cleveland, Ohio.

[27] *Home, Sweet Home*, 1863. Oil on canvas. 21.4 x 16.4 inches. National Gallery of Art, Washington, D. C.

[28, 29] *Defiance: Inviting a Shot*, 1864. Oil on panel. 12 x 17.9 inches. Detroit Institute of Arts, Detroit, Michigan.

[30] *Near Andersonville*, 1865. Oil on canvas. 23 x 18 inches. Newark Museum of Art, Newark, New Jersey.

[31] *Trooper Meditating Beside a Grave*, 1865. Oil on canvas. 16 x 8 inches. Joslyn Art Museum, Omaha, Nebraska.

[32, 33] *The Veteran in a New Field*, 1865. Oil on canvas. 24.1 x 38.1 inches. Metropolitan Museum of Art, New York City, New York.

[34] *Croquet Scene*, 1866. Oil on canvas. 15.8 x 26 inches. Art Institute of Chicago, Chicago, Illinois.

[36] *Paris Courtyard*, 1867. Oil on canvas. 17.1 x 12.1 inches. Maier Museum of Art at Randolph College, Lynchburg, Virginia.

[38, 39] *The Bridle Path, White Mountains*, 1868. Oil on canvas. 38 x 24 inches. Clark Art Institute, Williamstown, Massachusetts.

[40, 41] *The Trapper*, 1870. Oil on canvas. 19 x 29.5 inches. Colby College Museum of Art, Waterville, Maine.

[42] *Two Guides*, 1875. Oil on canvas. 24.2 x 38.2 inches. Clark Institute of Art, Williamstown, Massachusetts.

[43] *Artists Sketching in the White Mountains*, 1868. Oil on panel. 9.5 x 15.8 inches. Portland Museum of Art, Portland, Maine.

[44] *The Country School*, 1871. Oil on canvas. 21.2 x 38.2 inches. Saint Louis Art Museum, Saint Louis, Missouri.

[45] *Snap the Whip*, 1872. Oil on canvas. 21.9 x 35.9 inches. Butler Institute of American Art, Youngstown, Ohio.

[46, 47] *Three Boys on the Shore*, 1873. Gouache and watercolor on paper mounted on board. 8.6 x 13.6 inches. Terra Foundation for American Art, Chicago, Illinois.

[48] *Portrait of Helena de Kay*, 1872. Oil on panel. 12.2 x 18.5 inches. Thyssen-Bornemisza Museum, Madrid, Spain.

[49] *Shall I Tell Your Fortune?*, 1876. Private collection.

[50] *Dad's Coming*, 1873. Oil on panel. 9 x 13.7 inches. National Gallery of Art, Washington, D. C.

[52] *Moonlight*, 1874. Watercolor and graphite pencil on paper. Arkell Museum, Canajoharie, New York.

[54, 55] *Breezing Up*, 1876. Oil on canvas. 24.2 x 38.1 inches. National Gallery of Art, Washington, D. C.

[60, 61] *Blackboard*, 1877. Watercolor on wove paper. 19.7 x 12.7 inches. National Gallery of Art, Washington, D. C.

[64] *Sunset Fires*, 1880. Watercolor on paper. 9.7 x 13.6 inches. Westmoreland Museum of American Art, Greensburg, Pennsylvania.

[65] *Inside the Bar*, 1883. Watercolor and graphite on wove paper. 15.9 x 29 inches. Metropolitan Museum of Art, New York City, New York.

[66, 67] *The Life Line*, 1884. Oil on canvas. 28.6 x 44.7 inches. Philadelphia Museum of Art, Philadelphia, Pennsylvania.

[69] *Eight Bells*, 1886. Oil on canvas. 25.1 x 30.1 inches. Addison Gallery of American Art, Andover, Massachusetts.

[71] *An October Day*, 1889. Watercolor over graphite pencil on cream-colored wove paper (with scraping). 14 x 19.7 inches. Clark Art Institute, Williamstown, Massachusetts.

[72] *A Summer Night*, 1890. Oil on canvas. 30.1 x 40.1 inches. Musée d'Orsay, Paris, France.

[73] *Sunlight on the Coast*, 1890. Oil on canvas. 30.2 x 48.5 inches. Toledo Museum of Art, Toledo, Ohio.

[74, 75] *Hurricane, Bahamas*, 1898. Watercolor and graphite on wove paper. 14.4 x 21 inches. Metropolitan Museum of Art, New York City, New York.

[76] *Sunrise, Fishing in the Adirondacks*, 1892. Watercolor on wove paper. 13.5 x 20.5 inches. M. H. de Young Memorial Museum, San Francisco, California.

[78, 79] *The Adirondack Guide*, 1894. Watercolor over graphite on paper. 15.1 x 21.4 inches. Museum of Fine Arts, Boston, Massachusetts.

[80, 81] *Two Men in a Canoe*, 1895. Watercolor on gray laid paper. 14 x 20 inches. Portland Museum of Art, Portland, Maine.

[83] *Jumping Trout*, 1889. Watercolor over graphite on cream, medium-weight, moderately textured wove paper. 13.9 x 19.9 inches. Brooklyn Museum, Brooklyn, New York.

[84] *The Fox Hunt*, 1893. Oil on canvas. 37.9 x 68.5 inches. Pennsylvania Academy of the Fine Arts, Philadelphia, Pennsylvania.

[85] *The Fog Warning*, 1885. Oil on canvas. 30.2 x 48.5 inches. Museum of Fine Arts, Boston, Massachusetts.

[86] *The Gulf Stream*, 1899. Oil on canvas. 28.1 x 49.1 inches. Metropolitan Museum of Art, New York City, New York.

[87] *Right and Left*, 1899. Oil on canvas. 28.2 x 48.3 inches. National Gallery of Art, Washington, D. C.

[88] *Lost on the Grand Banks*, 1885.Private collection.

[90, 91] *The Lookout– "All's Well"*, 1896. Oil on canvas. 39.8 x 30.1 inches. Museum of Fine Arts, Boston, Massachusetts.

[92] *The Artist's Studio in Afternoon Fog*, 1894. Oil on canvas. 24 x 30.2 inches. Memorial Art Gallery, Rochester, New York.

[93] *Searchlight on Harbor Entrance, Santiago de Cuba*, 1901. Oil on canvas. 30.5 x 50.5 inches. Metropolitan Museum of Art, New York City, New York.

[95] *Cannon Rock*, 1895. Oil on canvas. 40 x 40 inches. Metropolitan Museum of Art, New York City, New York.

[96] *West Point, Prouts Neck*, 1890. Oil on canvas. 30 x 48.1 inches. Clark Institute of Art, Williamstown, Massachusetts.

[97] *Eastern Point*, 1900. Oil on canvas. 30.2 x 48.5 inches. Clark Institute of Art, Williamstown, Massachusetts.

EDWARD HOPPER

[100, 101] *New York Corner*, 1913. Oil on canvas. 24 x 29 inches. Cantor Arts Center, Stanford University, Stanford, California.

[102] *Night Shadows*, 1921. Etching. 6.8 x 8.3 inches. Metropolitan Museum of Art, New York City, New York.

[104] *Skyline, Near Washington Square*, 1925. Private collection.

[105] *Haunted House*, 1926. Watercolor on paper. 14 x 20 inches. Farnsworth Art Museum, Rockland, Maine.

[106] *The City*, 1927. Oil on canvas. 37 x 28 inches. Private collection.

[107] *Drugstore*, 1927. Oil on canvas. 29 x 40.1 inches. Museum of Fine Arts, Boston, Massachusetts.

[108, 109] *Automat*, 1927. Oil on canvas. 28.1 x 35 inches. Des Moines Art Center, Des Moines, Iowa.

[111] *Night Windows*, 1928. Oil on canvas. 29 x 34 inches. Museum of Modern Art, New York City, New York.

[112] *Freight Cars, Gloucester*, 1928. Oil on canvas. 29 x 40.1 inches. Art Institute of Chicago, Chicago, Illinois.

[113] *Manhattan Bridge Loop*, 1928.Watercolor and graphite pencil on paper. 14 x 20 inches. Whitney Museum of American Art, New York City, New York.

[114] *Early Sunday Morning*, 1930. Oil on canvas. 35 x 60 inches. Whitney Museum of American Art, New York City, New York.

[115] *House on Dune Edge*, 1931. Private collection.

[116] *High Road*, 1931. Watercolor and graphite pencil on paper. 20 x 28 inches. Whitney Museum of American Art, New York City, New York.

[117] *Room in New York*, 1932. Oil on canvas. 29.3 x 36.6 inches. Sheldon Museum of Art, Lincoln, Nebraska.

[118] *Room in Brooklyn*, 1932. Oil on canvas. 29.1 x 34 inches. Museum of Fine Arts, Boston, Massachusetts.

[120] *Cape Cod Evening*, 1932. Oil on canvas. 30 x 40 inches. National Gallery of Art, Washington, D. C.

[121] *Cold Storage Plant*, 1933. Watercolor and graphite on heavy white wove paper. 21.7 x 26 inches. Fogg Museum, Harvard University, Cambridge, Massachusetts.

[122] *Ryder's House*, 1933. Oil on canvas. 36.1 x 50 inches. Smithsonian American Art Museum, Washington, D. C.

[123] *House at Dusk*, 1935. Oil on canvas. 50 x 36.5 inches. Virginia Museum of Fine Arts, Richmond, Virginia.

[124] *Shakespeare at Dusk*, 1935. Private collection.

[125] *Toward Boston*, 1936. Private collection.

[126] *Mouth of the Pamet River—Full Tide*, 1937. Private collecdtion.

[127] *Compartment C, Car 293*, 1938. Private collection.

[128] *New York Movie*, 1939. Oil on canvas. 32.2 x 40.1 inches. Museum of Modern Art, New York City, New York.

[130] *Gas*, 1940. Oil on canvas. 26.2 x 40.2 inches. Museum of Modern Art, New York City, New York.

[131] *The Lee Shore*, 1941. Private collection.

[132] *Girlie Show*, 1941. Private collection.

[134] *Route 6, Eastham*, 1941. Sheldon Swope Art Museum, Terre Haute, Indiana.

[135] *Rooms for Tourists*, 1945. Oil on canvas. 30.2 × 42.1 inches. Yale University Art Museum, New Haven, Connecticut.

[136, 137] *Nighthawks*, 1942. Oil on canvas. 33.1 x 60 inches. Art Institute of Chicago, Chicago, Illinois.

[140] *Summertime*, 1943. Oil on canvas. 44 x 29.1 inches. Delaware Art Museum, Wilmington, Delaware.

[141] *Solitude*, 1944. Private collection.

[142] *Approaching a City*, 1946. Oil on canvas. 27.1 x 36 inches. The Phillips Collection, Washington, D. C.

[143] *Summer Evening*, 1947. Private collection.

[144] *Stairway*, 1949. Oil on wood. 16 × 11.8 inches. Whitney Museum of American Art, New York City, New York.

[135] *Rooms by the Sea*, 1951. Oil on canvas. 29.2 x 40 inches. Yale University Art Museum, New Haven, Connecticut.

[147] *Hotel by the Railroad*, 1952. Oil on canvas. 31.2 x 40.1 inches. Hirshhorn Museum and Sculpture Garden, Washington, D. C.

[148] *Morning Sun*, 1952. Oil on canvas. Columbus Museum of Art, Columbus, Ohio.

[149] *Office in a Small City*, 1953. Oil on canvas. 28 × 40 inches. Metropolitan Museum of Art, New York City, New York.

[151] *Road and Trees*, 1962. Oil on canvas. 33.5 x 59.5 inches. Philadelphia Museum of Art, Philadelphia, Pennsylvania.

[152] *Sun in an Empty Room*, 1963. Private collection.

[153] *Two Comedians*, 1965. Private collection.

Acknowledgments

BigCityLit: ("Edward Hopper's *Morning Sun,*" "Edward Hopper's *Night Shadows*");

Black Bough: ("Edward Hopper's *Cape Cod Evening,*" "Edward Hopper's *Drugstore,*" "Edward Hopper's *Office in a Small City,*" "Edward Hopper's *Rooms for Tourists*");

Blueline: ("Winslow Homer's *The Adirondack Guide,*" "Winslow Homer's *An October Day*");

Chaminade Literary Review: ("Edward Hopper's *New York Movie,*" "Edward Hopper's *Rooms by the Sea,*" "Edward Hopper's *Solitude*");

Cortland Review: ("Edward Hopper's *Early Sunday Morning*");

Dumb Beautiful Ministers: ("Edward Hopper's *Road and Trees*");

Ekphrasis: ("Arnold Newman's Photo of the Hoppers at Home in Truro," "Edward Hopper's *Approaching a City,*" "Edward Hopper's *Hotel by the Railroad,*" "Edward Hopper's *Skyline, Near Washington Square,*" "Edward Hopper's *Nighthawks,*" "Winslow Homer's *Moonlight,*" "Winslow Homer's *Snap the Whip,*" "Winslow Homer's *Sunlight on the Coast,*" "Winslow Homer's *Sunset Fires,*" "Variations on a Theme by Winslow Homer");

Ekphrastic Review: ("Edward Hopper's *Room in New York,*" "Winslow Homer's *Artists Sketching in the White Mountains,*" "Winslow Homer's *Bridal Path, White Mountains,*" "Winslow Homer's *Home, Sweet Home,*" "Winslow Homer's *Near Andersonville,*" "Winslow Homer's *A Sharpshooter on Picket Duty,*" "Winslow Homer's *A Summer Night*");

From the Farther Show: Cape Cod & the Islands Through Poetry: ("Edward Hopper's *Route 6, Eastham*");

Great Books Foundation Anthology: ("Edward Hopper's *New York Movie*");

Imaginary Museum: ("Edward Hopper's *Approaching a City,*" "Edward Hopper's *Cape Cod Evening,*" "Edward Hopper's *Gas,*" "Edward Hopper's *High Road,*" "Edward Hopper's *House at Dusk,*" "Edward Hopper's *The Lee Shore,*" "Edward Hopper's *New York Corner,*" "Edward Hopper's *New York Movie,*" "Edward Hopper's *Nighthawks,*" "Edward Hopper's *Room in Brooklyn,*" "Edward Hopper's *Rooms by the Sea,*" "Edward Hopper's *Rooms for Tourists,*" "Edward Hopper's *Office in a Small City,*" "Edward Hopper's *Road and Trees,*" "Edward Hopper's *Shakespeare at Dusk,*" "Edward Hopper's *Solitude,*" "Edward Hopper's *Sun in an Empty Room*");

Long Island Quarterly: ("Edward Hopper's *Night Windows,*" "Edward Hopper's *Road and Trees*");

Maier Museum of Art Journal: ("Winslow Homer's *Paris Courtyard*");

Moving Pictures (Shanti Arts): ("Edward Hopper's *The City*," "Edward Hopper's *Route 6, Eastham*," "Edward Hopper's *Freight Cars, Gloucester*," "Edward Hopper's *Haunted House*," "Edward Hopper's *Room in New York*," "Edward Hopper's *Stairway*," "Edward Hopper's *Summer Evening*," "Edward Hopper's *Two Comedians*" "Winslow Homer's *The Adirondack Guide*" "Winslow Homer's *Inside the Bar*," "Winslow Homer's *Moonlight*," "Winslow Homer's *An October Day*," "Winslow Homer's *Snap the Whip*," "Winslow Homer's *Sunlight on the Coast*," "Winslow Homer's *Sunset Fires*");

Paumanok: Poems and Pictures of Long Island: ("Edward Hopper's *Road and Trees*");

Poetry: ("Edward Hopper's *New York Movie*");

Poetry Bay: ("Edward Hopper's *Night Windows*");

Poetry East: ("Edward Hopper's *Manhattan Bridge Loop*");

Prevailing Winds (Shanti Arts): "Edward Hopper's *Summertime*," "Winslow Homer's *Artists Sketching in the White Mountains*," "Winslow Homer's *Bridle Path, White Mountains*," "Winslow Homer's *Croquet Scene*," "Winslow Homer's *Home, Sweet Home*," "Winslow Homer's *Hurricane, Bahamas*," "Winslow Homer's *A Summer Night*");

Thema: ("Edward Hopper's House at Dusk");

Things Seen: ("Arnold Newman's Photo of the Hoppers at Home in Truro," "Edward Hopper's *Automat*," "Edward Hopper's *Compartment C, Car 293*," "Edward Hopper's *Girlie Show*," "Edward Hopper's *Hotel by the Railroad*," "Edward Hopper's *Manhattan Bridge Loop*," "Edward Hopper's *Morning Sun*," "Edward Hopper's *Night Shadows*," "Nighthawks as Noir," "Edward Hopper's *Night Windows*," "Edward Hopper's *Skyline, Near Washington Square*," "Edward Hopper Painting Cape Cod," "Variations on a Theme by Winslow Homer");

13 Miles from Cleveland: ("Edward Hopper's Nighthawks as Noir");

Tribeca Review: ("Edward Hopper's *Girlie Show*");

Vermont Literary Review: ("Edward Hopper Painting Cape Cod");

Yankee: ("Edward Hopper's *Sun in an Empty Room*").

WINSLOW HOMER

A Sharpshooter on Picket Duty, 1862

Homer knew the horror
of a war not at all civil
that marked the start
of modern war unfair.

A captain described
the job of sharpshooting:
"only to watch and kill."

Stationed in tall pines,
a sharper's telescopic sight
could kill one mile away.

Sometimes a soldier,
gathering firewood,
abruptly fell dead.

"With everything as silent as the grave
here would come one of those rifled balls
and cut a hole clear through you."

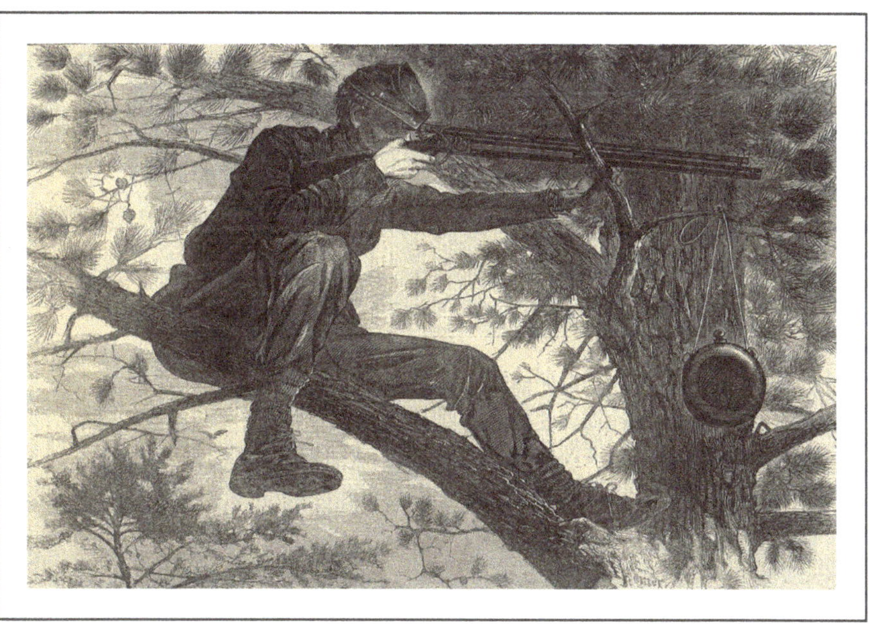

Winslow's Civil War Illustrations

In some of his war work,
Homer illustrated for *Harper's*
instances of what that *Weekly* wanted,
what they needed—

evocations of the war's ferocity
as depictions of Union gallops to victory,
even before the Yanks were actually winning,
but Homer was, himself, more interested

in campsite domesticities,
small moments where the men
were only lonely
sons and husbands.

Home, Sweet Home, 1863

Irony's at home here.
Ever so humble, indeed,
are the tiny tents of residence,
where a pair of soldiers sadly listen
to a regimental band,

discernable in the distance,
play the most popular of songs.

The soldiers' thoughts
wish away the war,
as they hear and re-hear
the bitter sugar sweet
chorus sound and repeat.

There's no place like home.
There's no place like home.

Defiance: Inviting a Shot, 1864

Homer's only picturing of a scene behind
Confederate lines wittily reveals two kinds
of fools. One crazily brave Reb
stands atop the trench, daring the Yanks

to kill him. On the distant Northern line
two puffs of smoke supply an answer.
Below this defiant, soon to be dead, man—
a comrade in Confederate gray

entertains his friends in black face—
polished features, reddened lips.
This fool strums a banjo to amuse his pals,
a cruel cliché that Homer thought

to be the essence of the defiant
idiocy that was the Rebel cause.

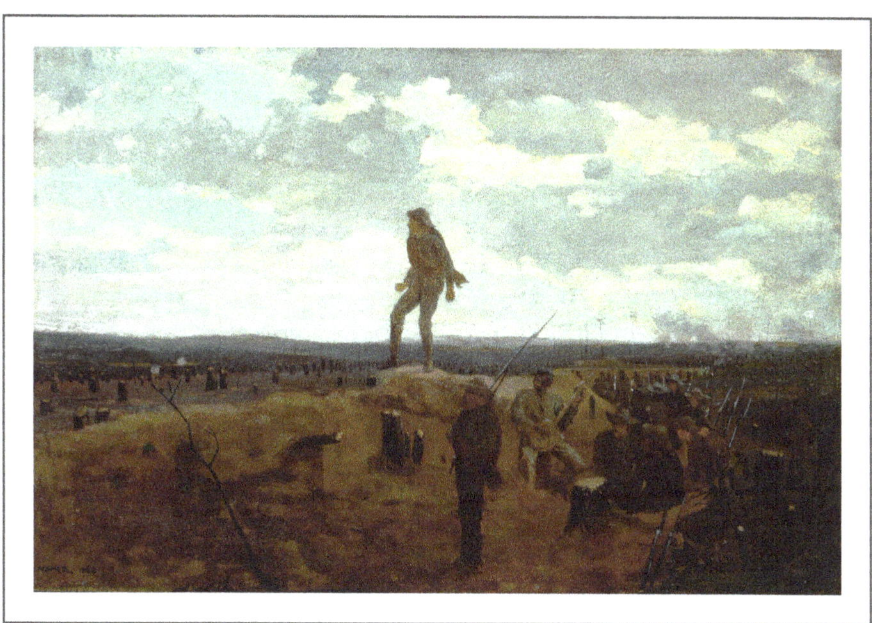

Near Andersonville, 1865

Homer was among the few who grasped
that the Civil War had three sides,
that slaves stood at a terrifying brink
shirts of grey or blue could not define.

This woman at the doorway
stands on more than one threshold,
and she is thinking, thinking, thinking
about her difficult world—

as, in the background, Reb soldiers,
their red flag drooping on a windless day,
march a long line of Union prisoners
towards the hell hole of Andersonville—

a shift in plot that does not,
for the prisoners
or this worried watcher,
bode well.

Trooper Meditating Beside a Grave, 1865

More than 750,000 died
in the Civil War, and
every dead man
was an American.

Homer's trooper
in this scene
wears a dark blue
Yankee jacket,

but his pants are
Confederate gray.
Homer wants to say
the toll fell hard

on both sides.
Grief was what all shared
Death was,
after all, the winner.

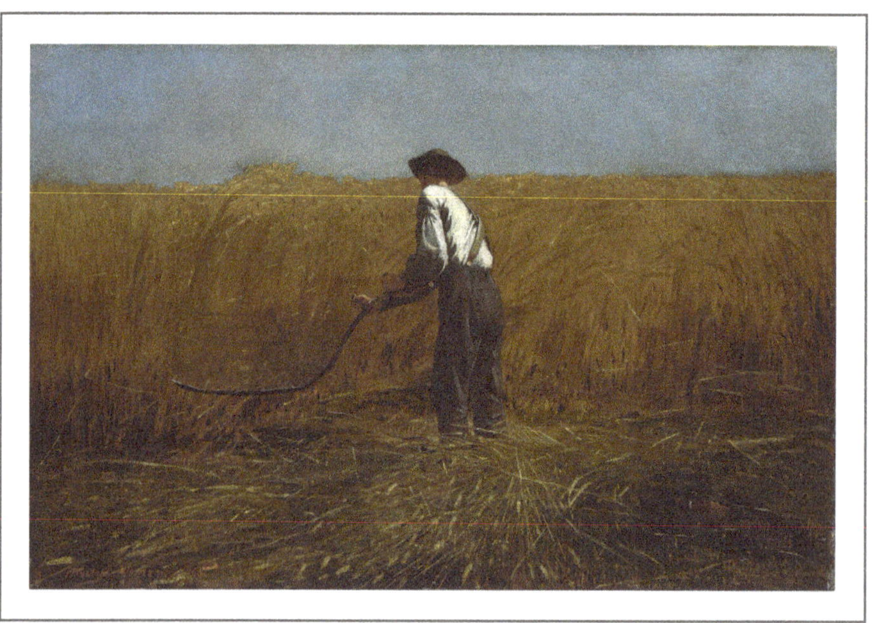

The Veteran in a New Field, 1865

The reaper—
a young, lean man just returned from War—
has discarded his dark-blue Union jacket
and his canteen, which bears the insignia

of the Army of the Potomac—
and bends to his work.
The wheat is extraordinarily high,
the record harvest of 1865.

This soldier, a Cincinnatus of sorts,
has decided, as Isaiah advised,
to swing a plowshare instead of a sword,
to put behind him the field of battle

and return
to the field of wheat.
As he swings his scythe, though,
we are reminded by a turn of thought—

a grim symbolism that will not let go—
that this reaper is fresh
from a harvest of death
he will never forget.

Croquet Scene, 1866

After the Civil War
Winslow often turned toward
a different sort of war,
a newly imported game women
could play as well as men.

Some claim women
played it much better than men.

And Homer, who loved women,
made a trio of lovely females his stars—
each gal a spectacular triangle of fabric
topped with a determined face.

Their faces for the game,
their "game faces" we might say,
declaring a desire to win the day,
despite the hampering
splendors of expansive gowns.

In this scene of croquet,
one man, who seems to be
Winslow his very self
is down on one knee
before a determined woman
in red attire.

Here's the joke:
his obeisance mimics
what could appear to be
a proposal to the lady in crimson,
but, in fact, he is merely
posing the ball of her opponent.
in a fatal position.

The woman in red is about
to clobber the ball
of the woman in blue.
to "croquet" it,
to knock it viciously away
towards the distant trees.

Homer, whose face we cannot see,
gives us only the top of his straw hat,
which makes him a mere zero
as he bends before
these gloriously gorgeous warriors,

who, oblivious to their own
all conquering beauty,
want only, at this moment,
to slap a wooden ball
victoriously
through a wire hoop.

Paris Courtyard, 1867

No one knows how Homer
passed his hours in Paris in 1867,
but we have a few paintings that show
what he might have
glimpsed or known.

This scene reveals
that he set his easel
left banked in a world where
to be voyeur was de rigueur.

A lovely girl, eyes downcast, demure,
hands crossed protectively to the fore,
passes through a courtyard.

Homer seems
to have liked
her shy demeanor—

he was to repeat her pose
after his return to New York,
giving us, a another look at her,

a lovely girl, eyes downcast, demure,
hands crossed this time
to carry a bouquet of flowers
in a field of wheat.

A Point of Turning

Living as an artist is seldom casy.
How can ends meet,
when sales are rare?

Winslow told his family
that the next exhibition could be his last.
It would be a test.

If neither of the two paintings sold,
he would give up on art,
the crazy career.

But both paintings sold
at the listed price,
and he vowed to forge ahead.

Decades later he discovered
his brother Charles had purchased
both pictures and stowed them in a closet.

When he finally discovered the trick,
Winslow grimaced and cursed under his breath—
his way of telling Charley he loved him, too.

Bridle Path, White Mountains, 1868

Back from Paris, Homer chose a new path.
A woman riding high in White Mountains
becomes his largest canvas,
and a place to pose a newly special friend.

He sketched a tourist on the trail. In studio,
his model is Helena on a chair.
On canvas he lends her a special glow.
She is for him the fairest of the fair.

She likes Winslow and loves his wit
and knows he sets her on this trail to star
in a tenderly affectionate drift
of thought: a bridal plan, that is, far

from what she wants from her master in art.
She knows this rocky ride may break his heart.

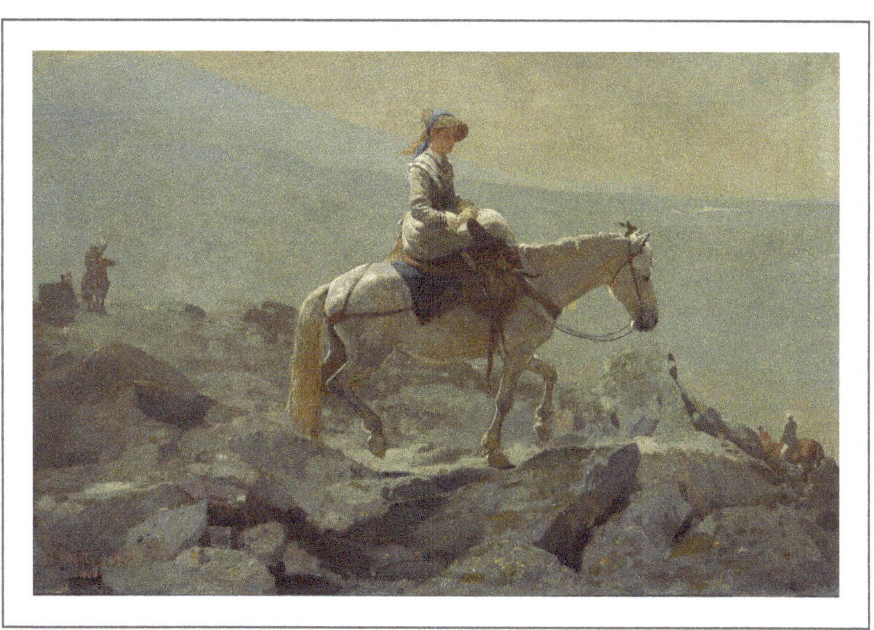

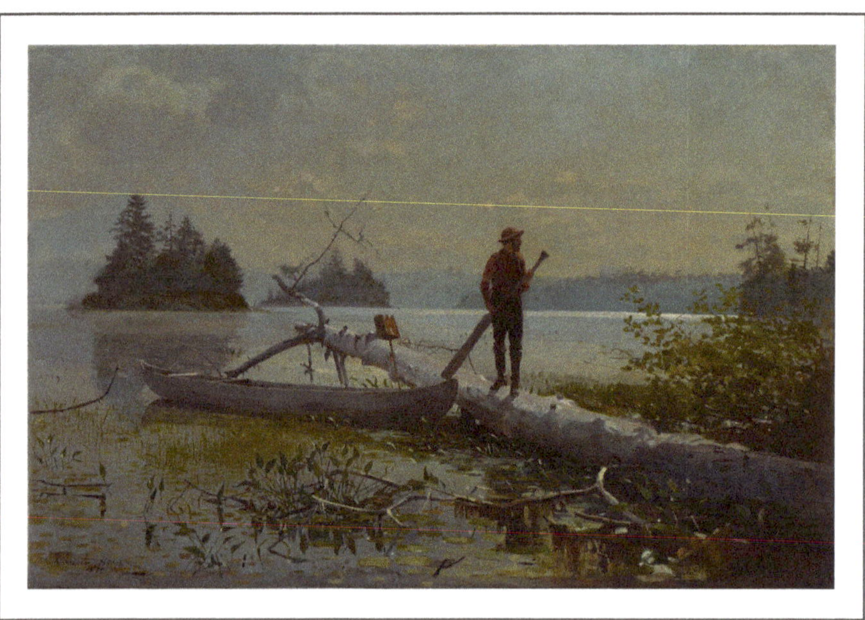

The Trapper, 1870

This is Homer's first capture
of his favorite Adirondack place.
Rufus Wallace poses for Winslow here,
as he so often would, over the years.

In this scene, the trapper balances on a log,
keeping his canoe in place
by means of extended paddle.
He turns to catch sight of something off-stage right.
The trapper—in exquisite balance and detail—
seems startlingly real.

That his figure is backlit gives the game away.
The specifics, too, speak to the value
of photo as preliminary sketch:
the perfectly rendered pickerel reeds,
the broken branches, the water lilies,
the carefully recorded serrations
of distant island pines, and the delicate line
of the fog-obscured shore.

This lovely naturalism reveals,
here more than in most of his pictures,
how well Homer learned
from the advice of LaFarge
and the example of Eakins
that a camera could be,
not often, but from time to time,
a means to truth—
that tremendous difficult thing.

Two Guides, 1875

A double portrait that is also a landscape
gives us kindred spirits.
Orson "Old Mountain" Phelps, as he was known
in the Adirondacks tourist books,
is pointing at something off in the distance.

His scruffy beard broadly surrounds
what we can see of his face
beneath his droopy brown hat.
He looks to be an angel whose halo
has fallen beneath his chin.

His companion, young Monroe Holt,
sports a bright red shirt and a jaunty little hat.
The fire-company shirt was thought
a deterrent to mosquitoes,
but for us it makes him a shout of color

in tune with autumnal foliage.
Holt gazes where Phelps points.
Beaver Mountain rises, triangular, behind them.
This pair seem caught in a moment of pause—
captured, we now know, by preliminary photo—

on a high ridge, laden with a carpet
of ferns and flowers—
weeds we might call them today,
but, for Homer, a display
of the sorts of wild things he loved to depict.

The flowers he often gave
as gifts of friendship.

Artists Sketching in the White Mountains, 1868

Landscape artists must be
part of what they see.
Homer's wry joke here gives us a line
of daubers in the midst of White Mountains—

each nattily dressed
but not at all a picturesque,
or sublime,
intrusion on the scene—

each with easel, palette, and umbrella—
unlovely against a lovely horizon
of clouds, mountains, and flowers.
The last of these sketchers

is Winslow himself
with his characteristic hat and mustache
and his name signed
on the backpack behind him.

That this is an occasion
for painterly camaraderie
as much as artistic productivity
is evident on the far left

where a bottle of wine
nests in a stump cleft,
coolly awaiting
the sun's set.

The Country School, 1871

The War killed off the men
so ladies took to teaching.

Homer spent a season watching children
at work and at play
under the watchful eyes
of beautiful young women.

As always, Winslow loved observing women.
In *The Country School* he shows us
a lovely lecturer tending all ages
in a one-room house—

girls to her left, boys to her right,
except for the tiniest and best-dressed boy,
who is crying and crying on the girl's bench.
An equally tiny girl watches him cry.

But the naughty tot's not
the only one who wants out.
The pretty teacher has paused her lesson
to gaze out the window.

We can see she yearns to put on her hat and depart.
(Her hat hangs on the wall behind her.)
But Homer records her sadly commanding stance,
and we can see she will stay the course.

Snap the Whip, 1872

Snap the whip is a game of run and fall,
of wanting to hang on but falling after all.
The running takes the boys towards
a goal that must be nothing in particular—

an open meadow, an expanse of flowers,
a distant mountain, a waiting schoolhouse.
The point of the game is holding on—
deftly, desperately—

but there would seem to be,
at last, no way to win, no way to lose.
The yank-back team is composed
of all who have fallen so far;

therefore this game, if not for weariness
or the end of recess,
could go on refining its fall and rise
until the end of time.

Three Boys on the Shore, 1873

This study in contrasts
asks blue and orange
to clarify as complements,

eloquent opposites,
redolent of *Chevreul on Color*,
the book Homer called "his bible."

The scenario, too, speaks of complementaries:
near and far as the balance
of space against time, time against space.

Near, but not face to face with us, the boys—
garbed mostly in blue and tan
but with, here and there, a bit of orange—

could be the three Homer brothers as children—
Charles at center, Winslow at left,
and Arthur inching up on the right.

They could be looking for,
as seacoast watchers often are,
something that's lost or might be found

The boys sprawl on orange flecked rock
gazing out at an absolutely blue ocean
whose horizon floats a sky—

clouds of white and clouds of orange
with a hint of softer blue that whispers:
distance has no end.

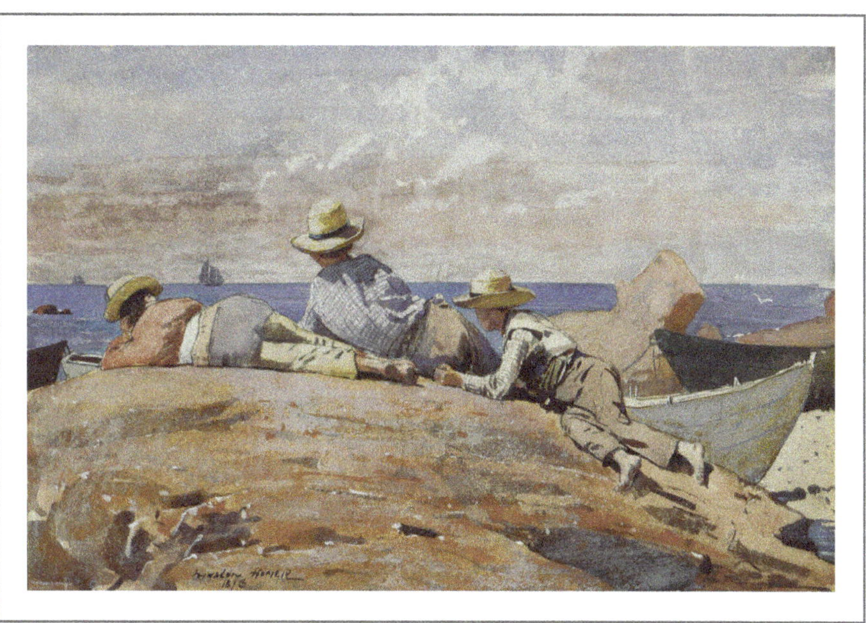

Portrait of Helena de Kay, 1872

He loved her, but she said no.
This picture speaks of loss,
and, yet, in spite of that, she glows.

The flower broken on the floor
denotes that she said no.
It seems she wants to rise and go.

She's looking down, her head is bowed.
Her mood is black as is her dress.
He loved her but she said no.

The artist knows she wants to go
and that she loves someone else,
but his colors embrace her,
and she glows.

Shall I Tell Your Fortune?, 1876

Helena sits on a hillside,
filling the frame with her intense gaze,
speaking her severe question
to the painter, her audience of one.

Her left hand presses
impatiently against her hip;
her right hand brandishes
the cards of misfortune.

Homer kept this peremptory portrait,
in his studio all his life.
He exhibited it only once,
at the venerable Academy in her city.

He must have wanted her to see it.
He painted into her hand
what he knew he was:
a jack at the mercy of a queen,

with other cards suggesting
details of failure and absence of grace.
A lack of diamonds in the cards
reveals prosperity was not his fate.

Dad's Coming, 1873

Absence was nothing new for Winslow.

His father was long gone
for most of Winslow's youth,
out West in luckless quest
for 49er fool's gold.
In later years, Winslow would need
to be caretaker-in-chief
for the declined,
at-last-returned, old man.

This picture enacts
a non-arrival
(despite its title)—
so sad the son,
perched on the tip of a beached boat,
gazing with rapt attention out to sea;
so sad the mother, clutching the heavy,
unsmiling baby,

as she glances down and to the side,
as if a spousal coming ashore
were the last thing on her mind.
Ironies redouble here:
the mom Winslow portrays
has the face of Helena de Kay,
the woman he had, just the year before,
loved and lost.

Absence was nothing new for Winslow.

Moonlight, 1874

A man and a woman reclining on a beach
facing a declining of the moon into the sea
could be a dream,
even a dream come true,

if they are lovers or in line to be,
but here we have the imbalance
of affection that most of us
have known or imagined or both.

This man adores this woman.
That much is clear.
The inclination of his figure
displays the inclination of his mind.

His face, too, is facing hers.
She eclipses for him,
it would seem,
this most resplendent moon.

But the woman tends the other way,
looking to the horizon for things to say.
Her open fan, unnecessary in the cool of night,
Seems poised to fend this fellow off.

When Winslow painted this picture
he was in full retreat in the Hamptons,
while Helena was off in the Big City
marrying her Gilder.

In this picture's frame,
Winslow keeps her in mind
for his fond fantasy's sake

(though she is entirely,
he is emphatically telling himself,
out of reach).

This one last water-colored Helena moment,
knows that moons must set
and waves on beaches break.

Breezing Up, 1876

When painting for the Centennial,
Homer decided to depict freedom
as three boys and an old man riding

a catboat on a breezy day,
heading home with a haul of fish.
The mast and the sail

lean out past
the edge of the painting.
It's as if the Homer boys—

Charles manning the rudder,
Winslow pushing out the sail with his feet,
Arthur just sitting and watching,

are in care of an imaginary grandfather,
glowing bright in a red shirt,
who firmly grasps

the line on the billowing sail,
making the wind do its work,
sailing the boys beyond the absence

that is the picture's edge.

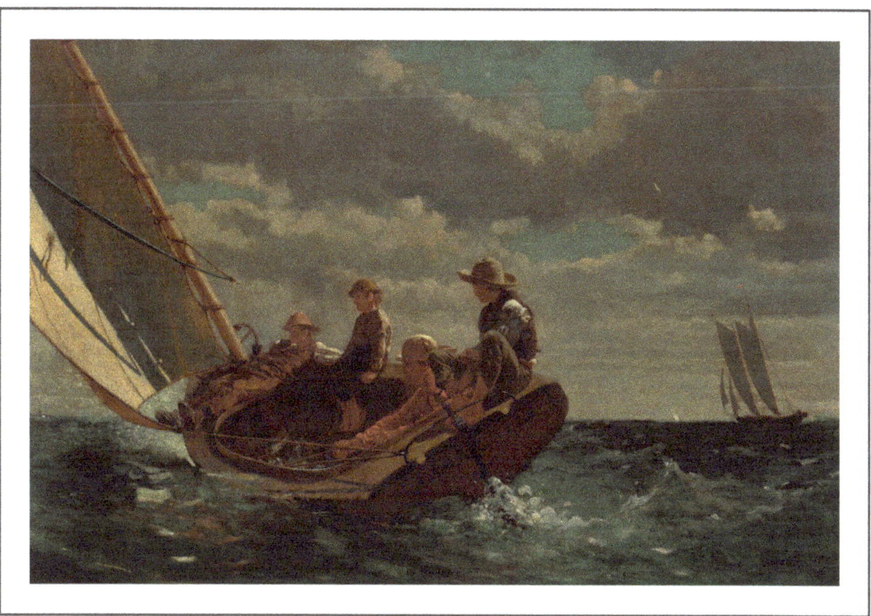

Winslow on a Porch in the South

Homer went South after the Civil War
to paint black folks in the fields,
in their homes, at their festivals,
at all sorts of places

Members of the Klan
noticed the actions
of this damned Yankee
and did not approve.

One afternoon as Homer sat
on his hotel porch, smoking,
an angry white guy hopped off his horse,
and, shotgun in hand,

strode menacingly towards,
the artist,
who remained calmly seated,
his hands in his pockets.

Afraid of what was about to happen,
another fellow on the porch
crouched down
in a corner, shaking.

Homer was to explain later:
"I looked the angry man in the eyes,
as Mother used to tell us
to look at a wild bull."

Half way down the path
the man hesitated, turned heel,
hopped back on his horse
and galloped off. "Why did he go away?"
Homer asked his companion,
who was just emerging
from under a bench.

"Well, the way you just sat there,
he must'a thought you had
a pair of pistols in your pockets
and were about to get the drop on him."

Winslow Tries on Whistler

In the year of the Centennial,
Winslow turned aesthetical
and depicted lovely ladies
in harmonies of watercolor—
pinks, oranges, yellows, sometimes grays.
Homer's Whistlerisms in the late 1870s

are surprising exercises in the Tonal.
Whistler, of course, pitched his tones
in higher keys than Homer
would ever want to go.
Whistler called his pieces
arrangements, nocturnes, and symphonies

and delighted in declaring them musical—
despite a lack of evidence
that a Whistler painting ever made a sound,
(let alone a musical one),
unless you consider the many occasions
when they were subject to noisy arguments

involving critics, patrons,
and, of course, the disputatious Whistler,
whose gentle art of making enemies
placed him at war,
even with Ruskin.
Homer took no part in such conversations.

It's not that he wanted to become Whistler,
it's just that Winslow could see that
the dapper expat's playful pieces
showed there was much
one could do
that was new.

Blackboard, 1877

This study in black and white and gray and beige
is a lesson in geometry in more ways than one.
The teacher, whose plaid gray apron
protects her long gray dress
has chalked shapes on a black board,
which is centered horizontally against a wall
that is beige above and dark gray below.

She stands on a horizontal expanse of beige floor.
The abstraction of what she stands before
is echoed by the way she stands in silhouette.
The long triangle of her body is topped
by the shorter, perfect triangle
formed by her left arm's grasp of her right elbow.

We can barely glimpse her right hand,
which points to the circle,
the one shape in her lesson
that is entirely lacking in angles.

At the bottom right of the board,
the artist's name appears—
signed, we are asked to believe, in chalk.
It's a march of straight lines
with one tiny "o" at its heart.

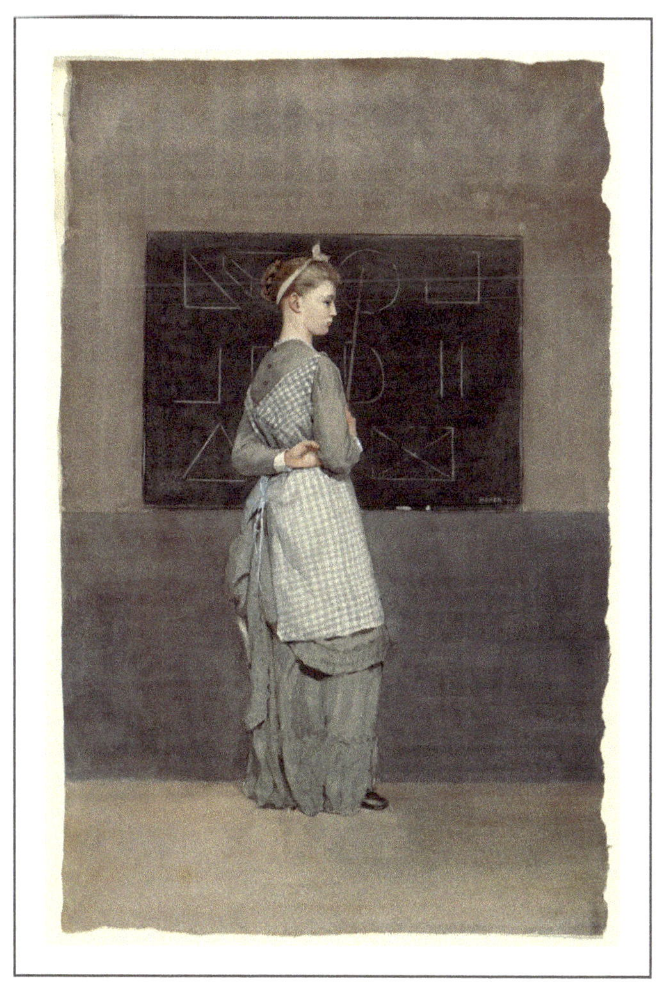

Winslow Painting at Houghton Farm

In 1878, Winslow nursed a melancholy
at his friend's farm in Mountainville
His watercolors there of boys and girls

featured, above all else, fences.
Sometimes boy and girl perch, precariously tandem.
More often, the fence comes between them,

a score for a sad song,
Homer playing boy against girl,
girl against boy,

tune and variation,
in scene after scene after scene all summer long.
In these rural repetitions we see,

again and again,
a shepherd Winslow failing to win
a shepherdess Helena.

These Upstate riffs on Jean Francois Millet
subtly speak, we might want to say,
to Helena's writings on *The Sower.*

Back in the City,
Winslow cast in tile
another lovelorn moment—

a shepherd, with hand on heart, looks sadly right;
a shepherdess, with hand on hip, looks sternly left—
a separation ceramic and never ending.

Sunset Fires, 1880

The dysfunctions of art
(those who want it do not want to pay for it)
underscore the dysfunctions of love
(a man without income cannot marry).

To be alone might be best, Homer decided,
so in 1880 he lived in a lighthouse at Gloucester—
a lighthouse is ideal for isolation
with water on three sides.

Water can be, he would always remember,
a buffer against all that's broken in heart or mind,
but water, too, with color added,
had become for him a means to catch the world,

even at end of day
when everything from sea to sky,
from horizon to shore,
seemed to be on fire.

Inside the Bar, 1883

At Cullercoats,
Homer saw women
as extraordinary.
A fishwife stands alone here,
staunch and steady
on a wave-rocked reef.

Her apron billows in high wind,
but she balances against it,
one arm akimbo,
the other holding the basket
the fishermen
will overfill with fish,
their coble approaches from the rear.

Though this occasion
could not be more ordinary,
Homer shows this woman to be
a presence gigantic,
her monumentality
connecting rocky shore and sky
and the sea that comes between.

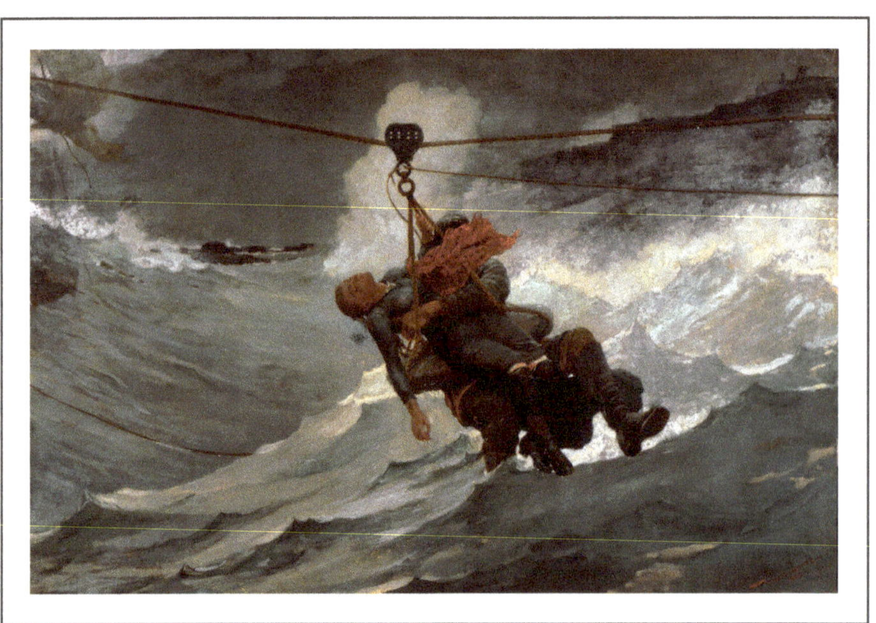

The Life Line, 1884

These two ride the sky, buoyed aloft—
their fate up, for now, in air,
above, mostly, the roil of waves.

We cannot see the man's face,
but he could be any man, every man.
The woman, though modestly attired,
is made curvaceous by a cling of clothes.

Off to the left the wreck
hovers in haze.
The boat's a ghostly lost cause.
A taut line stretches ship to shore,

leaving this pair safe in air—for now—
centered in scene, between rising waves
that enclose a dangling place, a ravine of mist.
Above the couple white water blasts, a climax of sorts.

This suspended animation wants
to speak only of a life saved.
This Cupid clasps his Psyche only to save her life;
and she settles in his arms only to survive,

The balance here is exquisite—
but somehow this rescue,
though proper in every respect—
suggests a ravishment.

In the distance, high up on the right—
distant, tiny watchers
wave their arms excitedly,
making the moment a performance.

Though necessity frames this embrace
it is, perhaps—for the so-long-lonely Winslow—
a dream about the one
who decided not to rescue him.

Eight Bells, 1886

Clouds have cleared,
and two sailors navigate,
sighting the sun
by check and check again,

their octants telling them
by angle of light
where the ship has gone
and where it should now go.

This navigation celestial
is an ancient means
to an end, and, indeed,
"eight bells" marks

the end of a sailor's watch,
and, in some songs,
such tolling serves
a purpose obituary,

homing a sailor to his hill.
Winslow, in 1886,
was sailing the dark passage
of his beloved mother's death.

He was charting celestial
through heavy weather.

Winslow Painting in the Tropics

In the tropics
Homer loved painting
the local black folks.
He shows them
constantly at work

at their gathering of turtles,
at their harvesting of coral,
at their diving for sponges,
at their fishing off their boats
(often for sharks).

The local whites are represented
only by their bleached walls,
which serve to keep the blacks,
away from the bleached houses,
away from the overflowing gardens.

When Homer shows the estates
of the rich whites it is only
to show black women and children
standing outside on the street
beside the gleam of bleached white wall.

On the tops of some of the bright walls,
we can see shards of glass,
the rich folks have cemented in place,
just in case someone of dark skin
has any thoughts about climbing in.

An October Day, 1889

A day in October can be lovely—
autumnal trees, rising as flaming verticals
against the green slopes of Beaver Mountain
and descending down the paper,
as reflections in
the bright blue of Mink Pond,

but, against this song of October glamor,
witness the hounding in its midst:
the hunter rowing the blue boat
towards a desperately swimming buck.

The buck fears the barking
of the determined dog on the far bank.
The hunter and the deer both know
the dog will not allow the deer
to come ashore alive.

As so often in Winslow's scenes,
we face a matter of life and death,
that insists upon a gorgeous world,
while never forgetting
there will be a meal in a hall
and a head on a wall.

A Summer Night, 1890

The two women are dancing in the moonlight,
twirling in between the glow of the house
and the gleam of the moon breaking on the sea—

turning and turning on the worn planking
of the porch that faces the rocky shore
where friends have gathered themselves
into piles of silhouettes

shored up against
the play of light whitening
the robin's-egg-blue sea
between grim gesturings of black rock.

This one's dreaming smile reminds him of Helena,
and Winslow suddenly sees
he must capture the wave spuming behind her.

Sunlight on the Coast, 1890

There is sunlight, we note, on the coast.

We see the sun declare its need to set
on the horizon just off Prouts Neck.
Its gleam breaks through clouds
as a swatch of bright where sea touches sky.

Light here tumbles on crests, foams in backwash,
flickers on slick edges of black rock,
and glows translucent blue
in a wave's gathering roll.

Homer knows that this painted light
is headed towards oceanic dark,
but he loves that its last moments
are everywhere apparent

as a withdrawal from one world
in behalf of the next
on a coast where light is endlessly broken,
ceaselessly repaired.

Hurricane, Bahamas, 1898

The buildings crouch before the storm,
but palm trees hold vertical
against the sheen of wind-driven sky,
each treetop an anxious asterisk of green.

Winslow loved coco palms.
His strokes of brush
define how pinnate leaves
curve to withstand a blast.

A slice of blue blue sea,
glimpsed at foreground left,
suggests the whipping wind
is not the story's end.

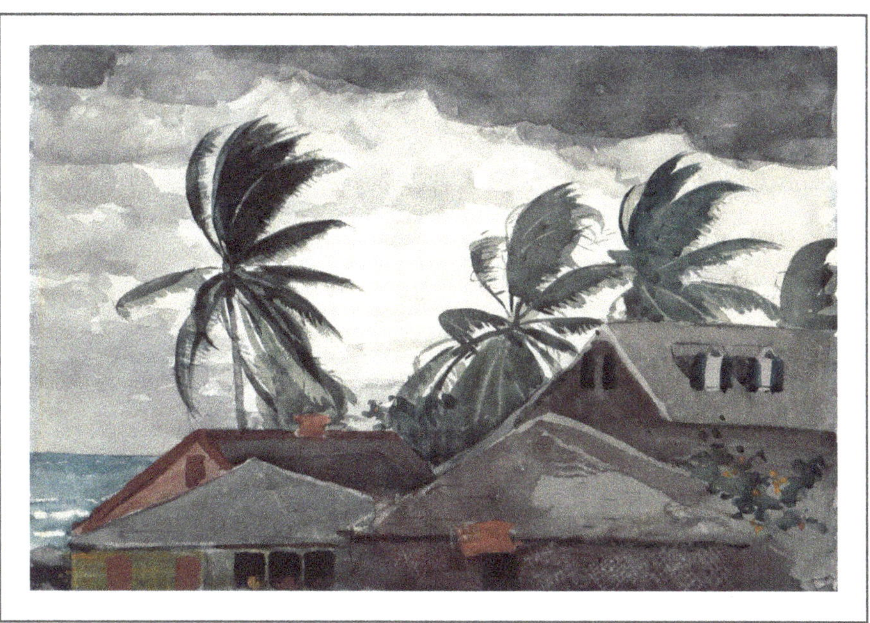

Sunrise, Fishing in the Adirondacks, 1892

Sometimes a trout will leap.
More often a small circle ripples,
revealing a rise of fish to surface.
From boy to man Homer loved fishing.
Again and again he cast
his watercolor brush

with a patience peculiar to anglers, trying to catch
the cool, subtly lighted darkness of early morning,
red striations of cloud adrift above

modulated green of mountain
and blackened sheen of water.
Homer caught, again and again,

the horizontal expanse of lake, sky, and mountain,
against which the depicted fisherman
casts his long, looping line across the scene.

Homer cut the line
into the paint
with the handle of his brush.

What he wanted was not so much
the fish hooked on the feathered lure,
but the moment before,

when line floats in air
above the disk of light
that marks the rise,

over which the fly drifts
tuned to the rhythm
that is this very fish.

The Adirondack Guide, 1894

Paper can take on water
for the sake of color.
In this watercolor the theme
might be, at bottom, water.

At top Homer floats
an Adirondack guide
crossing an Adirondack scene,
oars raised above a pond
that reflects a delicate sheen
of black, brown, and green.

We could say, too, that Homer
reflects on what it is
to be an old guy, wry and wiry,
isolate and emphatic of expression,
capped by a broken brown hat,
suspended in thought as well as on paper—

turning to us a sharp-nosed, bearded profile—
as if to say he knows damn well
what this moment
does not need to mean.

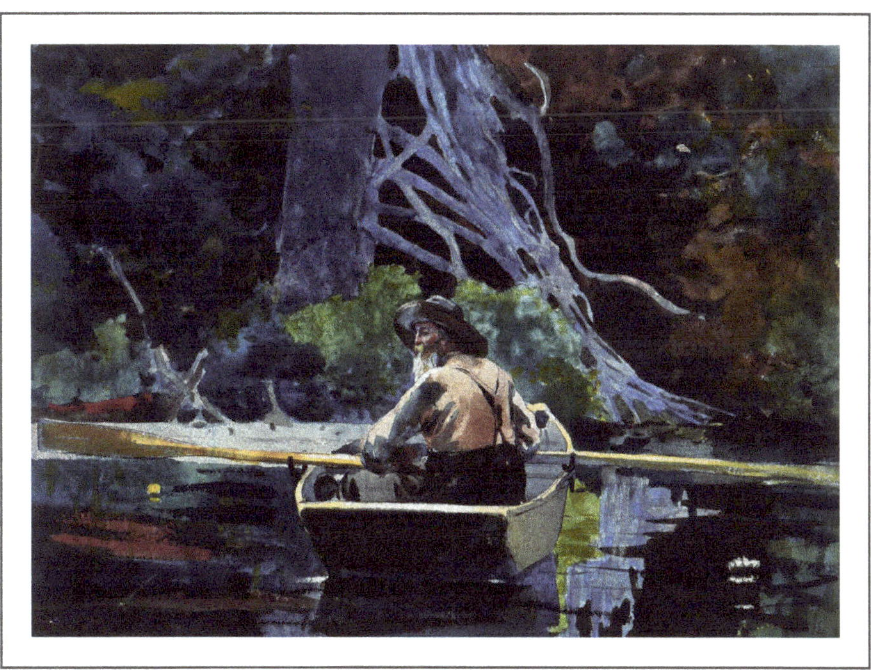

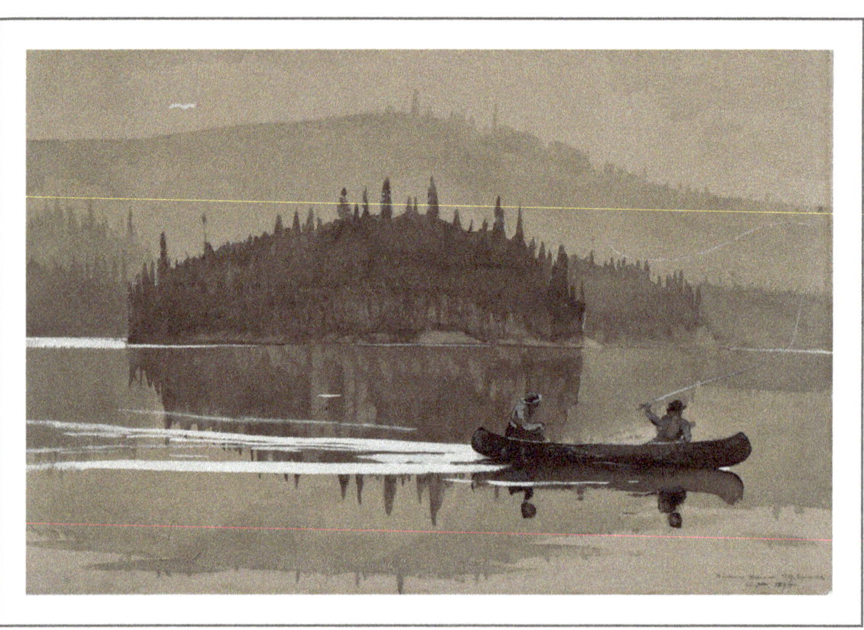

Two Men in a Canoe, 1895

In Quebec, Homer turned to monochrome
to perform the subtleties of Lake St. John
where the ouananiche lift towards the sun,
and, each day, before the fish rise,
a pair of anglers, Charles and Winslow,

were up and at them, floating their canoe across
a silver expanse of chiaroscuro.
It's all, Winslow knew, a matter of tone,
where black and gray and white can
be all the colors, or, at least enough of them

for this fragment of dawn
with its still unseen sun subtly
stroking land and water,
while sharp verticals of distant island pines
pluck a kind of counterpoint,

a pizzicato horizon line
that echoes the drift of the two men across
a continuo of water lapping against hull.
We watch them cast their crafted, and crafty, flies
towards what is rising or might soon rise.

Winslow Trout Painter

Homer painted few portraits of people,
but when it came to trout
he could not resist depiction.

Trout are fine folk.
They are brave and strong and honorable;
and there is no need to sell them pictures.

Then, too, they can be
quite tasty.

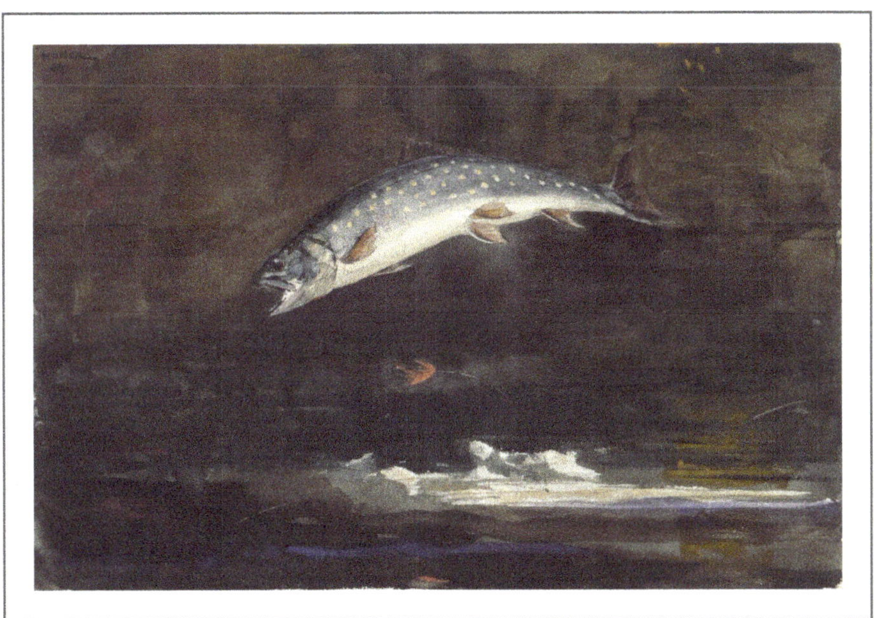

Variations on a Theme

1. *The Fox Hunt*, 1893

A fox—
harried in snow by a gathered hunger
of crows—

echoes Homer's name,
cornered on canvas.
Both fox and name

appear as ruddy diagonals
determined to keep on going,
lunging desperately

through the white fear's
spectral brushwork
that the artist's name

and his animal
cannot rise
above.

2. *The Fog Warning*, 1885

The fisherman's home races
across
in the distance,
searching,
anxiously,
for him.

It is about to be lost to view
in the horizon's rumor of fog
that may soon be
the only thing
he can see.

3. *The Gulf Stream*, 1899

The waiting is
all he has
to hold onto

besides the stalks of sugar cane,
sweet last straws to grasp
in hopes that help might come.

Even now a phantom ship
teases the horizon—
one of the dreams

he'd have to be
unframed to see.

4. *Right and Left*, 1899

Two ducks suspended in mid-air
above angry green waves.

One, bullet-struck, dives to its demise;
the other, about to fly away,
will have to live without its mate.

Neither life nor death,
neither right nor left,
the artist tells us,
is entirely without fear.

Lost on the Grand Banks, 1885

The stance of this pair of fishermen,
as they stare at the clouted horizon,
captures a purity of fear,
but there is nothing they can do,
nothing they can say.

They can only look and hope and pray.
The direction their ship,
or any ship, might come
they have no way of guessing.
The fogged darkness surrounds them.

Their tiny boat is tossed
and on the brink of swamping.
A heavy surge rises
as they look
the other way.

Their one caught cod curls
in the stern. Its head seems
to scream towards the sky.
A pointless anchor protrudes
like a small crucifixion at the bow.

The oars hang useless on the sides.
The foreground oar reaches out
towards the angry green of the sea,
as if pleading for help
or mercy.

In 1998, Bill Gates paid 30 million
for *Lost on the Grand Banks*.
Why would the richest man in the world
want to hang fear
on his wall?

Maybe the rich have the means,
despite opaque skies,
to see what's coming.

The Lookout—"All's Well", 1896

This face is in our face—
an absurd close-up for a declaration
whose implications
echo and re-echo.

It's an assurance
doubly sure
that can only be
an exercise in irony.

Homer understood
as well as anyone
that "all" is never ever
entirely and absolutely

"well."

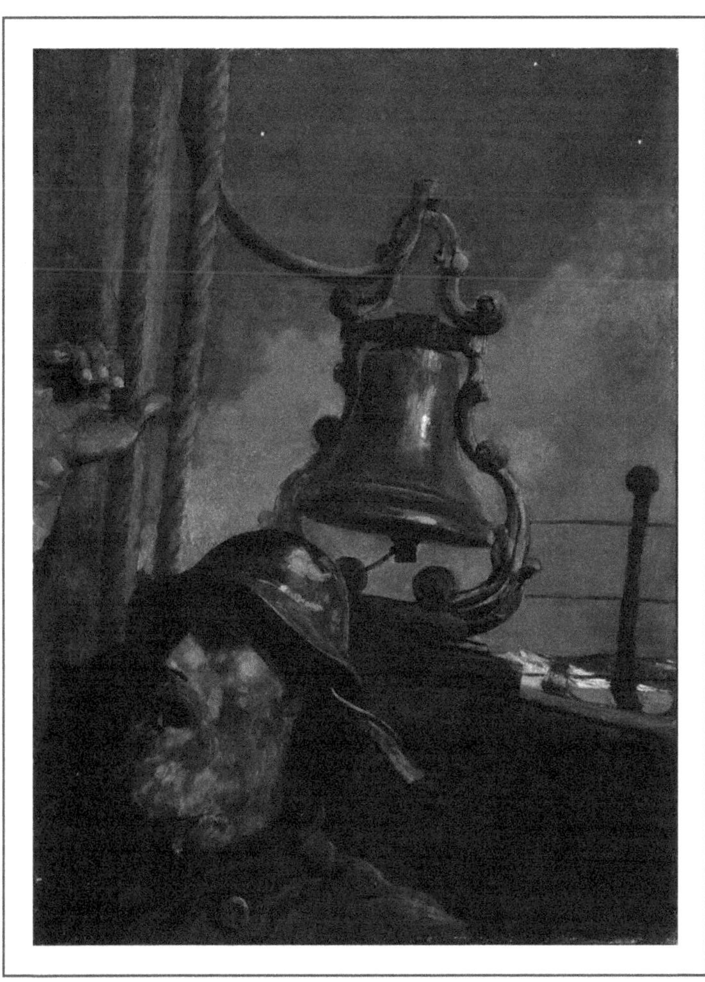

The Artist's Studio in Afternoon Fog, 1894

A portrait of self:
this depiction of his place at Prouts Neck,
his haven from the wider world,

silhouetted in distant view,
obscured by fog and cut off
by a diagonal rocky ledge,

gives us a glimpse of a home
that does not let us in,
does not want us there.

This painting's a way for Homer
to hold his world in mind—
a view within,

and yet without, too,

that captures a whisper of the balcony
where he daily witnessed
sea and sky.

This picture speaks to itself,
more than to us
of a life

silhouetted and held dear.

Searchlight on Harbor Entrance, Santiago de Cuba, 1901

A terrible,
now mostly forgotten,
war was fought in this harbor.

Homer, we know, was saddened
by the many lives
lost here.

The Spanish ships down there then
were helpless against
the barrage of fire power.

Two cannons remain.
The moon floats, half full,
above the castle

The strobe
of the electric searchlight,
finds nothing beyond

the dark blue of the sky
and the lighter blue of the sea,
but it tells us

by its silently endless reach
that the 20th century has dawned
and all the nothings we see here

will keep on gleaming,
cruelly,
beyond all lines of horizon.

Winslow Big Game Hunter

Winslow loved fishing all his life,
but his take on hunting was more complex.
Though he rendered scenes of the sport
for his audience of hunters,

his sympathy seemed
more with the deer than the hunter.
Death was, after all,
the powerful undertow of his art,

the fate all must face, on sea or land.
In woods, he armed himself
with pad and pencil,
his weapons of choice.

Still, there was that hunt in 1908,
near the end of his life,
when he and his friends came face to face
with an angry bear.

As the big beast charged
and his companions froze in fear, Homer,
after quickly sketching the creature,
seized a rifle, aimed, and fired,

killing the animal with one shot.
His only non-fish entry in the Club log,
in the many years of his visits there,
was recorded by the artist

in a large, firm hand:
"Winslow Homer, 1 Bear."

Winslow's Triptych

Homer wanted three seascapes hung together.
They embodied, for him, Prouts Neck.

1. *Cannon Rock*, 1895

Cannon Rock,
depicts the spot below his studio
where a rocky cropping aimed always out

and to the left of the rolling waves.
Every day he observed the distinctive rock
and often scrambled, at low tide, to stand upon it.

Those of us who visit his studio seek out Cannon Rock.
It is the barrel Homer sighted down towards the sea,
the moving target that was so often in his sights.

Necessarily beyond his reach,
the sea was the fleeting thing at which
he needed to take aim.

2. *West Point, Prouts Neck*, 1900

Walking west of Cannon Rock,
he found this scene
"fifteen minutes after sunset—
not one minute before."

He returned to the spot again and again,
striving to get this end of day exactly right.
It angered him that some critics
found this painting's color lurid.
This swerve of water
bursting before the bleed of sunset
reveals, he was sure,
precisely how a day dies.

3. *Eastern Point*, 1900

Walking east of Cannon Rock,
he found a stretch of brown shore
fronting a black bar of reef.

The ocean roars and breaks
on both these jags of rock,
cresting before the high winds

and drifting eastward
against
the always darkening sky.

EDWARD HOPPER

New York Corner, 1913

This saloon faces
a murderous expanse
of intersection.
Let's drink
to that.

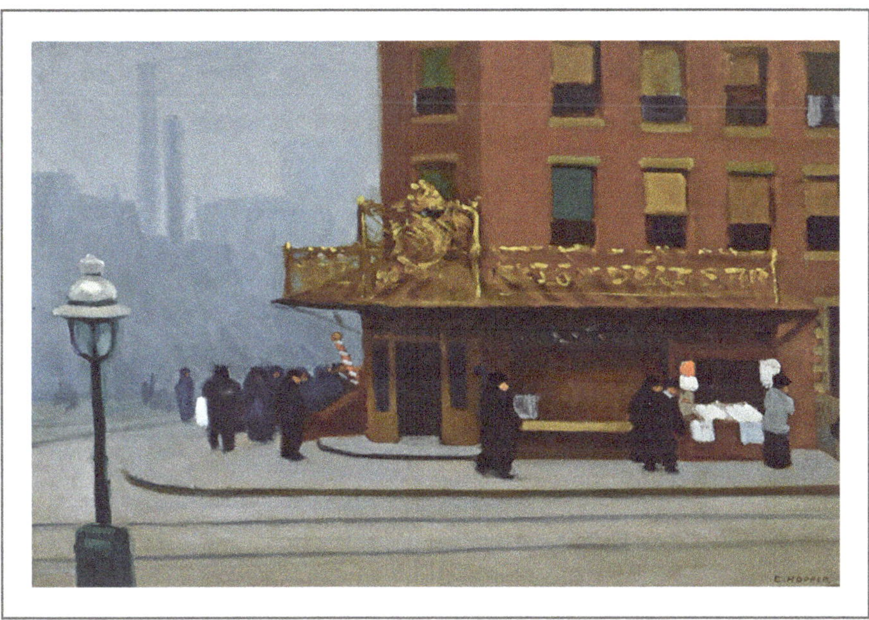

Night Shadows, 1921

It is early in the century but late at night.
Hopper has leaned out an upper-floor window.
He is looking down at the sidewalk
and the facade of the business on the corner.
A tall, unseen pole casts a long shadow
that a man is about to walk into.
I want to imagine this man my father,
though that makes me a conception
whose time has not yet come.

In '21 he has not even met my mother.
On this paper street his foreshortened form
is a small gathering of ink,
deposited by intaglio, etched to adhere,
where he strides in a hurry.
Centered on the horizontal,
he is the point of balance
that implies the immensity
of New York City night.

One man walking—solitary, ordinary—
going nowhere in particular,
passing without giving the matter any thought
under the spotlight
of a brilliantly lighted, nondescript corner,
towards shadows
that will keep going
all the way
to the unseen stars.

Skyline, Near Washington Square, 1925

He puts on too brave a facade,
and having lost his companion to fire,
he stands isolate and absurd.

His top story too starkly articulated,
wearing his row of Doric pilasters
like an excess of epaulets,

he stares back at us,
stricken and striking,
across the intervening roof line,

which cuts off,
from our point of view,
his head.

Haunted House, 1926

A haunted house, an emptied shell,
stands against a gray day in 1926.
Broken windows, a scattering of holes,
hint the house is beyond what tools can fix.

Hopper paints the shadows of the dormers
as gorgeous rows of purpled blues,
revealing how light can render
unexpected felicities of hue

and inexplicable solidities of shape.
Meanwhile subtle inflections of darkness
reach long limbs down a sloping grade,
shadow arms that hint of a grasping ghost.

A little joke Hopper whispers;
his house haunted by his laughter.

The City, 1927

A corner of a square is a view
to look down upon in 1927:

this clash of architectures startles,
a striking cacophony

centered on a monstrously lovely Victorian verticality,
its decoratively mansarded façade

up rising through the picture's heart.

Drugstore, 1927

A drugstore window
in 1927:
jarred red light and blue
islanded in the silent street—
one war ahead, one war behind.

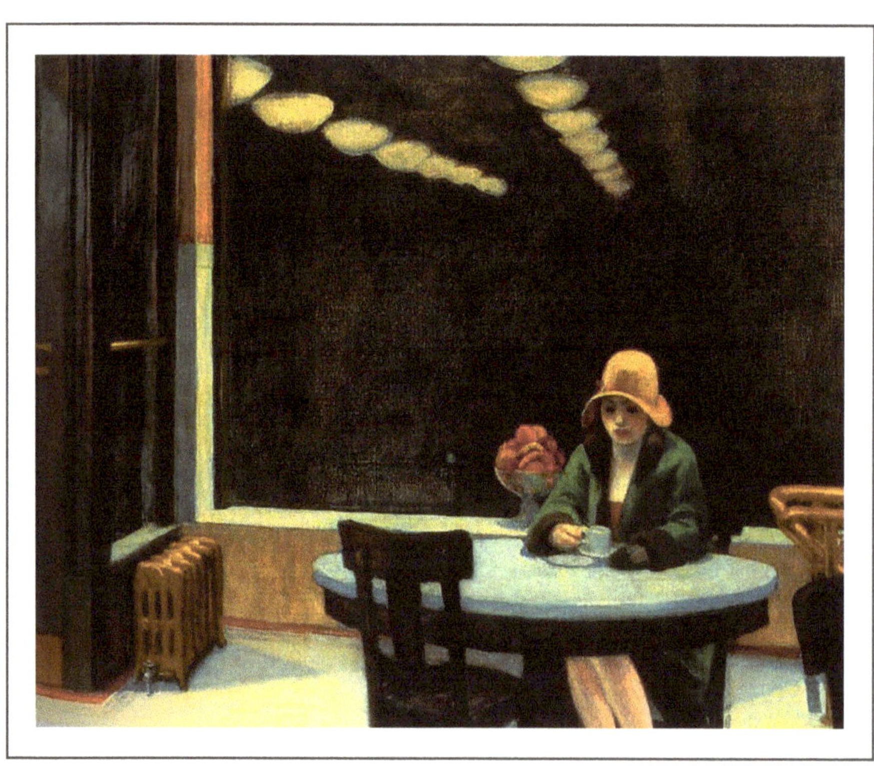

Automat, 1927

The day conveyed a daily round of tasks
from her desk to the next and on and on.

Nothing seemed started, nothing seemed done.
A moment of peace is now all she asks,
as she seats herself by herself, alone
with her thoughts but not lonely—no, not that.

She's full of what her life might be, what
her lover whispered when he saw her home.

For us she is a thing that Hopper made—
a still life, a life stilled—an arrangement
frozen just shy of 1928,
whose respite is, for us, her fate.

Lighthouses

Hopper loved lighthouses.
They are, like Hopper,
isolate and very tall.
Yet they were to him
more than self portraits--
though they were that, too.

In *Portland Head Light*, for instance,
he shows how light can inhere
in the blued blond
of a seaside tower,
rounded, beautifully,
by darkened shadow.

Though a lighthouse
stands alone,
it gestures towards
those who face
the dangers of a place
where waves meet rocks.

As in so many of his works,
Hopper sings fears
as the merest whispers.
Bright lighted and geometrical,
these prospects for the disastrous
speak sotto voce,

as if it they are only
the sun
on the side of a building.

Night Windows, 1928

The picture is all about
what the surrounding absence
makes of light
inside where the woman dwells
with her window open for air,
undressed
to her final grace note,
her pink slip.

Naked almost
she knows herself to be
but thinks she has held herself
inside a private moment in 1928,
primping
for what she hopes
her night will bring.

Held tight to her only life,
she's not in the least aware
of what Edward Hopper
manages to see,
riding the evening El,
accompanied by
those crude voyeurs,
you and me.

Freight Cars, Gloucester, 1928

The foreground grass flickers bright in gold and green.
The burgundy freight cars remain on track;
they are the mid-ground stars of Hopper's scene.
Married four years now, Eddie and Jo are back
again painting in their honeymoon spot.

At right angles to the trains and Gloucester roofs
a sun-smacked pole holds up the picture's top.

Jo's figure remains unseen in this view—
she's down by the harbor painting the boats
with her old pals—artistes of nothing new,
like Jo, not destined to be of note.
Yet Jo's on Eddie's mind. His strokes of fire,
the foreground grasses strike and strike again,
suggest, at bottom, he's not without desire.

Manhattan Bridge Loop, 1928

Even though the complex, oddly lovely facades in the background
are bravely facing down
the cruel fullness of the slanting light,
it is the horizontal in the middle ground
Hopper wants us to witness:
a bridge that could go on and on forever, looping
by the insidious implications of cropping,
while one lone workman,
who is slashed across the shoulders by a swath of light
and who could be the only man alive,
strides purposely towards the edge of the world,
his back mostly towards us,
trying to get off.

Early Sunday Morning, 1930

Nothing stirs on Seventh Avenue but light
and color, red so red and green so green,
notes that complement the bright
harmony the mind strives to see,
a long-shadowed Manhattan morning,
a subtly melodious 1930
of windows and doors that sing
a broad expanse of street,

but no one seems to be at home here
except the woman painted out in window four,
whose ghosted life returns now as pentimento,
as she suddenly throws open her window,
and cries,
"Oh, come in, come in my dear.
It's been so long, and we have missed you so!"

House on Dune Edge, 1931

On the dune's edge
a round turret of a house
is a fitting outpost,
a snug place
to hold a soul inside,
a bastion of sorts
against the harsh winds and seas
of Cape Cod in June 1931.

In a photo
taken in 1984,
we can see that,
somewhere,
behind the new rooms and trees,
the old turret—
if not the dune or its edge—
lingers.

High Road, 1931

Every high road hangs up somewhere in air,
an instant of paused overview we overlook
as we pass down the white-blue
slash of concrete between yellow fields

of dry-hot summer's unrelenting light—
scenes so hard-edged they cannot be real
but cannot be anything else.
All roads lead to what they cut through

and never stop till they reach the sea,
the neverending low road,
and the sky,
the neverending high.

Room in New York, 1932

Seated in the room's one comfortable chair
a husband hunches forward, intent upon his paper
as if his life depended on the scores he finds there.

Just home from work
he has not yet loosened his tie,
nor spoken with his wife

who is wearing her bright red dress,
the one with the bow in back that
comes easily undone.

She knows he has not noticed
so she plunks the keys of her piano
to say to him softly

that she is there
and has been waiting all day
for him.

The room glows—
yellow walls, oak table and door,
the rosy tones of the man's chair and the woman's dress.

Something could come of this.

Room in Brooklyn, 1932

High in the air of New York City
is a pale, blue sky and a light
such as could be anywhere
over cornfield or mountain peak.
When the steady, steely breeze,
dampened by ocean and river,
has done its work, there is something
almost clean to the high sky.
Up where the many have their rooms
there is a sweetness to a morning
slant of light tall windows let in.

In such moments it matters not
that bay window faces no bay.
Row on row of red brick provide
a kind of landscape, rooftops bristling
with shallow forests of pipes and tanks.
There is wilderness and ruin enough
to such a view to free the heart
for a moment of ecstatic calm.

Neither Wordsworth with his abject abbey
nor Friedrich with his crumbling gorge
could ask for more than this, really.
The dark-haired woman in a dark-blue dress,
a Romantic of another sort,
has placed fresh pinkish white flowers
in a milk-white, fake-alabaster vase.
The supple curve of the vase catches
the brightness of the light and makes
it into a womanly shape,
modeled by delicate shadow.
It is almost as if the woman
had placed her own lovely body,
of which we can know nothing,
out for the sun and Edward Hopper
to reflect upon. The illumined shape
is an idea entirely in our eyes—
or in hers, perhaps, should she look up
from her book and her mind's line of sky.

Cape Cod Evening, 1932

The moment's center
sees a dog poised in tall grass,
ears tuned to autumn's
stiff breeze: he sniffs bitter air
as is if it were just weather.

Cold Storage Plant, 1933

These pinks and tans
shape a grim,
jagged mass of warehouse
that has nothing going for it
beyond the way
the open jaw it brandishes
seems bent on swallowing—
the light-blue sky and the dark-blue sea—
purposed as these buildings are
for absolute storage
of cold.

Ryder's House, 1933

"I can hear the silence,"
one critic said of this intersection
of, seemingly, doorless boxes

that form a dwelling
solid as stone—

offering us no way in,
no way out.

House at Dusk, 1935

At dusk we cross a magic line
between seeing out and seeing in,
A subtle proscenium

open on both sides
of an intangible now,
weighs the question—

who is seen and who is seeing?—
with so delicate a balance
that all who come and go

and all who come to window
share a twilit romance
never shown to be known,

except in the dusky French verses
Hopper adored,
where inscrutable swans glide

and no one touches anyone,
though the evening, vast and tender,
makes a kind of love out of only light,

only light.

Shakespeare at Dusk, 1935

Here we see the twilight of a day
Edward Hopper painted Central Park
until the darkness sealed it all away.

Before the colors slipped into the dark
he penciled names: cream, sulfur, and mauve;
Shakespeare's base he fated to be chocolate.

"Sunset intense" he wrote and set afire
the painted sky that came from this late
afternoon in late nineteen thirty-five.

The trees were ruined choirs except for one
bright maple in the middle distance, alive
with scarlet light, a deft fragment of song.

Toward Boston, 1936

His watercolors bear whatever crosses there are,
omitting, almost always, the wires
that might carry our messages—
mine to you,
yours to me.

He bares two crosses here,
enough for two thieves,
but you will find no savior between them,
only a tiny railway station,
vintage 1936,

that once sheltered those
in South Truro
who were on their way
to whatever Boston had to offer
or just come back.

Mouth of the Pamet River—Full Tide, 1937

The sheen on the water sings
the fall of dusk
on a pale yellow house,
an odd nub of habitation
caught between

the road's swerve,
the rail track's delicate diagonal,
the utility pole's crucifixion,
and the interflux
of river and full-tide sea—

all seen in failing, brilliant light.

Compartment C, Car 293, 1938

Compartment C is almost all about green—
the color of the illusory, the fleeting,
the never to be attained,
the sweet spring seasons always out of reach—
a color he usually saves for accents, notes of grace.

Jo here is looking sexy—
in the preliminary drawings it is clearly her—
though the woman in the finished painting,
as so often in Hopper's scenes,
is Jo re-imagined as dream.

New York Movie, 1939

We can have our pick of seats.
Though the movie's already moving,
the theater's almost an empty shell.
All we can see on our side
of the room is one man and one woman—
as neat, respectable, and distinct
as the empty chairs that come
between them. But distinctions do not surprise,
fresh as we are from sullen street and subway,
where lonelinesses crowded
about us like unquiet memories
that may have loved us once or known our love.
Here we are an accidental
fellowship, sheltering from the city's
obscure bereavements to face a screened,
imaginary living,
as if it were a destination
we were moving toward. Leaning to our right
and suspended before us
is a bored, smartly uniformed usherette.
Staring beyond her lighted corner, she finds
reverie that moves through
and beyond the shine of the silver screening.
But we can see what she will never see—
that she's the star of Hopper's scene.
For the artist she's a play of light,
and a play of light is all about her.

Whether the future she is
dreaming is the future she will have
we have no way of knowing. Whatever
it will prove to be
it has already been. The usherette
Hopper saw might now be seventy,
hunched before a Hitachi
in an old home or a home for the old.
She might be dreaming now a New York movie,
Fred Astaire dancing and kissing
Ginger Rogers, who high kicks across New York
City skylines, raising possibilities
that time has served to lower.

We are watching the usherette and the subtle
shadows her boredom makes across her not-quite-
impassive face beneath
the three red-shaded lamps and beside
the stairs that lead, somehow, to dark streets
that go on and on and on.
But we are no safer here than she.
Despite the semblance of luxury—
gilt edges, red plush,
and patterned carpet—this is no palace,
and we do not reign here, except in dreams.
This picture tells us much
about various textures of lighted air,
but at the center Hopper has placed
a slab of darkness and an empty chair.

Gas, 1940

It is late. This chance may be our last.
Although we know we need much more than gas,
this opportunity must not slip past.

The narrow road ahead will not go fast;
it curves into a dark-forested mass
of trees. This chance may be our last.

The day is done, the last, long shadows cast.
Summer's gone, and autumn's seared the grass.
We know this seasoned hour will not last

and should not go unnoticed, overcast
by thoughts of things that never came to pass,
opportunities that slipped by in the past.

The Mobil pumps must be secured, locked fast.
The owner wonders if we will bypass
him here. He knows this chance may be our last.

His station will stay lighted till we've passed.
When he shuts down, the darkness will be vast.
It is late. This chance might be our last,
an opportunity we might decide to pass.

The Lee Shore, 1941

Seen from a certain
angle of grief
a house could seem
almost a way to sail
out to sea.

Girlie Show, 1941

Puritan by birth, sensualist at heart—
Hopper was struck by something
he wanted to say on Valentine's Day, 1941,
while gazing at a buxom woman,
disrobed and prancing,
on the last stage of the Minsky family's
grand wheel of burlesques
in the old Republic on 42nd Street.

Fed up with Fiorello
and The Little Flower's tedious complaint
against displays of flesh
and wanting to say so in paint,
Eddie asked Jo to pose for him
again and again—
their studio on the top floor
of No. 3 Washington Square North
become a theater runway,
another round in the game they played,
Jo posing, actress that she was,
for another of Eddie's many women.

The first sketch of her in conté crayon
very tenderly rendered
her fifty-year-old body,
nude and lovely,
her arms raised in the stance
of the dancing Girlie,
her legs gaily striding,
her face turned toward the artist,
squinting at him as if to say,
"Is this enough, Eddie,
can I stop now PLEASE,"
shivering but holding her pose,
her firm breasts upturned to a degree,
her loveliness especially lovely for him,
as he keeps her in this difficult pose
for his own joy,
and hers, too, if truth be told,
in the intimate Times Square
of their intensely complicated
intersection.

Route 6, Eastham, 1941

After Hopper designed a scene,
he'd plan his colors.

His notes for this picture place
"pale green" on one wall,
"pale warm grey" on another,
"pale lavender" on still another.

His shadows tumble in one direction
as "dark warm lavender"
and as "cold shadow" in the other.
All he wanted, he once said,
was to paint sunlight
on the side of a building.

Here we see him flicking on
Cape Cod light
one color at a time.

Rooms for Tourists, 1945

Sometimes
all we need to know about
cozy, bright rooms is
that we have been
left outside.

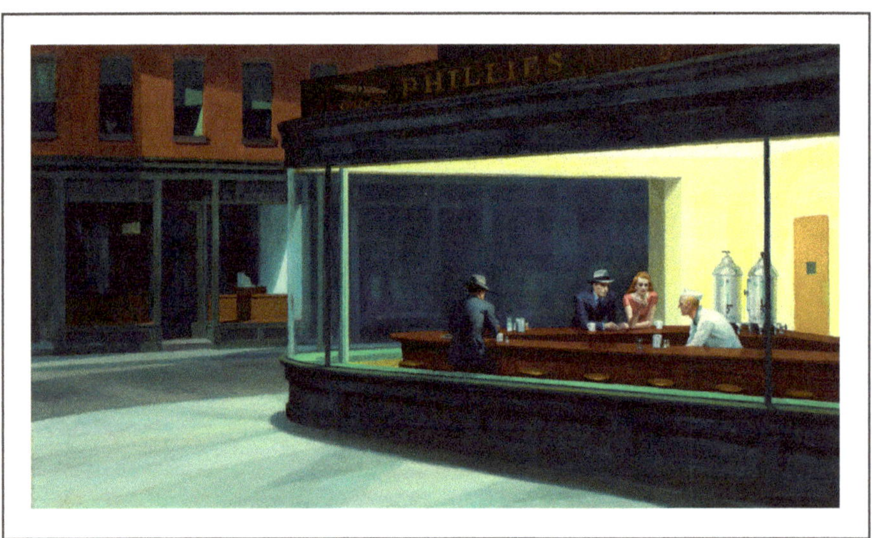
PHILLIES

Nighthawks, 1942

It is about 11 p.m. It is 1942. Edward and Jo have just seen *The Skin of Our Teeth*, off-Broadway. They have sought the solace of a cup of coffee and a moment's respite before the five-block walk back to Washington Square. They have been here before and can call the counterman by name. They sit near where he works at the slicings for tomorrow's sandwiches, knowing he will ask about the play. They want to talk about it. Edward found it funny. Jo thought it sad.

The man across the counter is Mr. Antrobus, disguised as Thornton Wilder, but the Hoppers know nothing of this, nor that this scene is a continuation of the play, nor that it will become Edward's most famous picture.

Edward and Jo talk about the Antrobus children and think, without sharing their thoughts, about the Hopper children that will never be.

Jo rides the high stool, turning over and over a matchbook that says "God is love" on both sides. Edward's right hand, holding a cigarette, rests on the counter a fraction of an inch from Jo's left hand, but they do not touch.

The café is a cool slice of fluorescent light jutting into the darkness that is New York City night. It is the prow of a ship riding the ghosted blue of doorways and the long, dangerous green of alleyways—shoals of shadow.

The war is everywhere and nowhere. The casualty lists in the evening paper tick off the seconds till dawn.

Mr. Antrobus/Wilder—missing his haunted, imaginary domesticity—shoves his *Times* into his coat pocket, leaves a tip, and leaves. He is thinking he will ride the last train out of Penn Station to a little, nonexistent suburb in New Jersey, where, in a little house near a pond, a little family he will never have waits crouching around a fire, while dinosaurs thunder down suburban streets and the terrible, ridiculous cold comes on.

Nighthawks as Noir

—for Tony Quagliano

It was a scary scene, and I didn't want any part of it.

I could tell that the big man,
sitting alone three seats to my left, down the long café counter,
was casing the joint and up to no good.
He was well dressed, sure,
but too well dressed for this joint at this hour,
sporting a Norfolk jacket and a natty vest
you'd hardly notice because he'd buttoned up so tight.
He was clearly not a guy given to small talk.
You could tell he would shoot you as soon as talk to you,
but that bulge in his pocket and the stains on his hands
gave the game away,
telling me more than I wanted to know
about how he made his dough.

He was an artist all right, probably a painter
from the look of those colors under his finger nails.
That bulge under his coat had to be a fully loaded sketch pad,
a dangerous weapon in the wrong hands.
Every so often he'd yank it out and scratch away
for a few minutes then tuck it back in his pocket.
I could see the couple across from him—
the red-haired dame and her hawk-nosed beau—
were getting nervous and wondering what he was up to.
I figured I'd better get out of there, while I still could.
So I set my glass on the counter and left.
You can see it there still,
if you care to look,
up there on a wall in Chicago.

Summertime, 1943

Hopper, the supposed Puritan, offers us here
a strawberry-blond almost nude.
Her thin blue-white dress
hiding next to nothing.

Because the pale hue
of her frock echoes the gray-blue
of discretely concrete architecture
in summer light,
everything on view
seems, at first to sing
a monochrome of stone,
a cool harmony of calm,
but there burns
at the heart of the scene
a passionate aria,
that thrills
to a covertly revealed blond body
(really Jo's figure in disguise),
bra-less breasts glowing
through a painterly
pretense of linen.

The building's door,
gaping wide behind her,
offers another sort
of warmth of tone—
as sensuous in its own way as the woman—
the red-brown wood of its opened frame
whispering
a vaginal dark.

Solitude, 1944

The sadness of horizon
is a matter of perspective,
the point being the vanishing
where lines converge
only because we see them to.

That vision is delusion
saves us from nothing.
Seeing's myth
conceals a truth:

though there is no point
to vanishing,
we will all vanish anyway.

Approaching a City, 1946

The way into the city is a darkness
that opens to a shadowed underground.
These are thoughts we approach but do not express.

With so much ahead we try to think of less,
knowing how clocks will turn us round and round.
The way into the city is a darkness

that remembers what we cannot confess:
that shadows shape what our lives have found.
A thought we can approach but not express

suggests that the future must be a guess—
a lie we must pass through or go around.
Yet the city's inclination to darkness

should come as no surprise and no distress.
The light that strikes against wall and ground
is a thought we approach without express

prospects for joy or grief or tenderness,
keeping in mind the sky's pale-blue surround.
There is no way into the city's darkness,
which we have approached but not expressed.

Summer Evening, 1947

On the porch of Hopper's childhood home
in Nyack on the Hudson
a memory shapes a picture.

His sister, Marion,
who will never marry;
listens to a young man tell her something.

What he is saying does not make her happy.
Nothing explains her dismay or how this scene
turned the rest of her life against her

and away from the earnest young man;
turned her into the spinster sister
of a famous painter.

Stairway, 1949

This stairway
takes us down
to a doorway
open far too wide
to a brooding mass
of shadowy trees—

one of Hopper's
favorite jokes:
a path
we cannot help
but take
that leads
only
to dark.

Rooms by the Sea, 1951

A house that opens wide its door
to an open expanse of sea is more
than a machine for living, and less.

This opening to an abstract wedge of blue
makes the infinite an idea of horizon
that casts on floor and wall a sad, finite

hexagram of pale oceanic light—
a heightened palette's subtle alchemy,
white become gold, that we must see to glow—

a trick, but also a joke—
a piece the painter knew would be called
abstract and surreal and real, too.

Still,
a scene must be a life—
trick, joke, and all—and we can see

that someone has lived here,
around the frame's corner
and into the adjoining room,

where the faded rose of the sofa rises
to dispute the brown smudge of the bureau.
Everything they say they have said before.

Even the worn green rug knows their songs
by heart and will not listen
as the threadbare, angry voices rise and fall.

Meanwhile, the waves outside the dreaming doorway
have their own voices. "Mine, mine, mine," they cry
as they break against each other.

Hotel by the Railroad, 1952

Though we do not speak, there seems to be a harmony here.
The blackened blue of my vest and pants echoes
the blue of the chair in which Jo hunches
reading her dark-blue book. All these things
refer, too, to the somber blues, lightened by ocher,
of the shadows on the wall of our dismal room
and the wall of the windowless building
my gaze cannot avoid considering as I stare
across the burgundy tracks that echo, in turn,
the burgundy of the mirror's frame.
Then there is the forest green of the almost unseen
carpet and the window shade glimpsed around the corner

and the bright yellow, modulated with white,
of the curtains and the hotel's outer walls.
The tracks—which, again, I appear to gaze on,
poised as I am, thinking about all this,
while my cigarette burns almost down to my fingers—
are painted entirely burgundy, for the sake of my scheme,
for the sake, as I have said, of the harmony,
despite the real steel such tracks have always shown me.
These tracks slice past the edge
of where we seem to have stayed the night
in a hotel we will be leaving soon to ride parallel lines,
despite Jo's evident anger, out of this scene and into another.

Morning Sun, 1952

"A vast and tender / peace / seems to descend / from the heavens . . ."
—from a Paul Verlaine poem Edward Hopper gave to his wife, Jo

This harsh light seems a kind of voyeur.
She faces it through an open window,
a light that is the gaze of her only Edward
basking on her, his one and only Jo.
With a marriage that seems a kind of war,
how can they stay so devoted, so true?
Attired in the red-orange he'd a passion for,
she's held in his mind's box of green and blue.
He's made her echo the red-brick horizon
that gleams beneath the sky across the street.
Facing the rise of a new day's sun,
she opens to rumors of light and heat,
but the vast, descending peace her lover
has shaped around her seems entirely untender.

Office in a Small City, 1953

Some offices
take us so high
light
is all we
ever see.

Arnold Newman's Photo of the Hoppers at Home in Truro, 1960

Hopper stares us down
in early morning light,
hunched and implacable.

Awkwardly seated
with his arms winged outward on both sides,
he grips the armrests of the white chair,
as if he were about to propel himself upward,
to rise to his feet
to leave us and Arnold Newman
staring only at his house
whose roof line echoes the spread
(because he hasn't left us yet)
of Hopper's arms.

The huge north-facing window of the house
seems to float above the painter's head
like a cartoon balloon,
waiting to be filled with the grim sunlight
of his thoughts,
while to the side of the house,
outlined against sea and sky,
we can just make out the tiny figure of Jo Hopper
(managing, as she always did, to get into the picture)
gesticulating wildly.

Road and Trees, 1962

The trees form a line of dark green beside
the gray roadway. The sun's
lowering light breaks ocher and aquamarine

against the two trees that face the decline
of the afternoon.
The road shoulder closest to us catches more

of the bright, showing grass-green with patches
of brown. A pale-blue band
of sky is creamed over with cloud in one corner.

We never see the road this way. We are always
only on it, headed somewhere
or at an end and getting off. We never

keep in mind the ordinary sight
and what having it
has meant to us alive to our passages.

Everywhere here light dances
with its absence,
the shadows that have so much to offer.

Sun in an Empty Room, 1963

The sun is silent in the empty room;
the window shapes it into panes of light.
The painter knows he will be dying soon.

The slanting rays betray no trace of gloom.
This seeing sings the joys of sight,
the sun silenced in the empty room,

its pale, glimmering squares whistling no tune
beyond grace notes of yellow and white.
The painter knows he will be dying soon,

but finds comfort in the green afternoon
that hints of a greener world, off-stage right.
With the sun silent in the empty room

we wait in vain for the room to become
more than an inn for the light:
the painter knows he will be dying soon.

He shows us his absence from the afternoon
in the shadows that make us see the light—
the sun, silent in the empty room—
the painter knowing he will be dying soon.

Two Comedians, 1965

Eddie was 83, sick and slowing
towards an ending when he painted
himself and Jo taking a last bow
on a stage commedia dell'arte.

In early sketches he is Harlequin,
the trickster dressed in diamond designs,
the guy who always wins
over death and all else,

and Jo alone is garbed in Pierrot white,
the uniform of the fool—
who, because of innocence and a kind heart,
always loses.

In the end, though,
Eddie painted himself
in white, too, accepting, it seems,
the inevitable sweetness of defeat,

but he retained his dark trickster hat,
as if he'd kept at least
one more trick up his,
ostensibly white, sleeve.

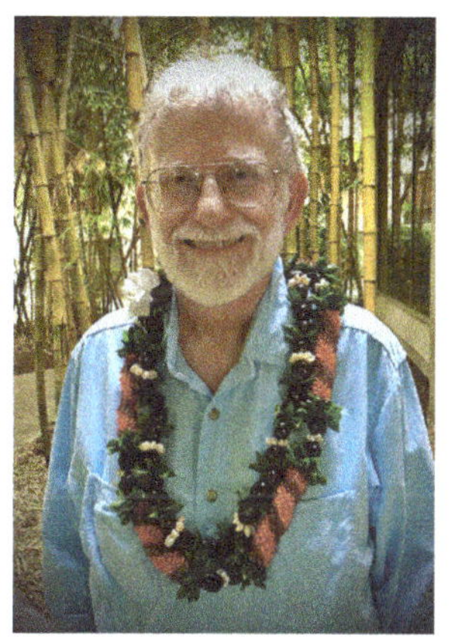

Joseph Stanton's previous books of poems are *Prevailing Winds, Moving Pictures, Things Seen, Imaginary Museum: Poems on Art, A Field Guide to the Wildlife of Suburban O'ahu, Cardinal Points*, and *What the Kite Thinks: A Linked Poem* (co-authored with Makoto Ōoka, Wing Tek Lum, and Jean Toyama). His other books include *Looking for Edward Gorey, The Important Books: Children's Picture Books as Art and Literature*, and *Stan Musial: A Biography*. His poems have appeared in *Poetry, New Letters, Harvard Review, Antioch Review, New York Quarterly*, and many other magazines. As an art historian, Stanton has written about Winslow Homer, Edward Hopper, Edward Gorey, Maurice Sendak, and other American artists. He has collaborated with artists, musicians, and other writers, and has received many awards for his work, including the Tony Quagliano International Poetry Award, the Cades Award for Literature, and the Ekphrasis Prize. Professor Emeritus of Art History and American Studies at the University of Hawai'i at Mānoa, he continues to teach in varied settings, most recently teaching the Starting with Art poetry workshop at Poets House in New York City and at the Honolulu Museum of Art.

www.ingramcontent.com/pod-product-compliance
Lightning Source LLC
LaVergne TN
LVHW052353100826
845147LV00013B/832

9781956056891